WARRIORS
DON'T CRY

A Searing Memoir of

the Battle to Integrate

Little Rock's Central High

THE EXCHANGE

**How can the
media unite
or divide us?**

WARRIORS DON'T CRY

A Searing Memoir of
the Battle to Integrate
Little Rock's Central High

MELBA PATTILLO BEALS

Abridged Edition

Handwritten annotations:

Memoir | Autobiography
- covers specific time frame | - covers whole life
- uses sensory details

HAMPTON-BROWN

- zero in on a specific moment + zoom out
- has a theme

From WARRIORS DON'T CRY by Melba Patillo Beals. Copyright © 1994 by Melba Beals.
Reprinted with permission of Simon Pulse, an Imprint of Simon & Schuster Children's Publishing Division.
All rights reserved.

Front cover photos: students © by George Silk/Time & Life Pictures/Getty Images; flag © by Digital Stock.
Back cover photo: flag © by Digital Stock.

On-Page Coach™ (introductions, questions, on-page glossaries),
The Exchange, back cover summary, cover design © Hampton-Brown.

Hampton-Brown
P.O. Box 223220
Carmel, California 93922
800-333-3510
www.hampton-brown.com

Printed in the United States of America

ISBN-13: 978-0-7362-3170-1
ISBN-10: 0-7362-3170-6

07 08 09 10 11 12 13 14 15 10 9 8 7 6 5 4 3 2

I dedicate this book to the eight brave and gentle warriors with whom I attended Central High School in 1957:

Elizabeth Eckford
Ernest Green
Gloria Ray Karlmark
Carlotta Walls LaNier
Minnijean Brown Trickey
Terrence Roberts
Jefferson Thomas
Thelma Mothershed Wair

and to our mothers, fathers, and family members who supported us through this incredible experience

Acknowledgments

I am grateful to:

the late Supreme Court Justice Thurgood Marshall—our guiding light, our protector—a brave warrior whose tenacity and courage will be an inspirational banner to mankind for all eternity.

Federal Judge Robert Carter, like Justice Marshall an untiring architect of the *Brown* v. *Board of Education of Topeka*, Kansas decision, also a warrior who has forged a path with his own life.

L. C. Bates, Daisy Bates, Wiley Branton, Sr., and the ministers who stood beside our parents to cheer us on.
Federal Judge Ronald Davies—a man with the courage of his convictions.

the brave men of the 101st Airborne who guarded us.

the memory of the late Eugene Smith, and to all Little Rock police officers who risked their own lives to shield us from the mob.

Grace Lorch and Benjamin Fine, who gave comfort to Elizabeth in the face of a mob.

Mrs. Pickwick, my shorthand teacher at Central High, who exhibited a sense of fair play.

Elizabeth Huckaby, girls' vice-principal at Central High, who tried to give Personal Best.

the very few nameless Central High students who dared to smile or cast a pleasant glance or refused to torture us.

Link, who dared to be my friend.

George and Carol McCabe, the white surrogate parents who took me into their home, gave me unconditional love, and walked with me over the bridge to adulthood.

Judy, Joan, Dory, and Rick McCabe, who welcomed me as their sister.

my spiritual family, always at my side when I needed them: Aliaster and Consi Smith; Maria and Jean Picard; Sanford and Catherine Rosen and family; Dr. Mimi Silbert; Babette Wurtz, and Dr. David Geisinger.

my dear sisters and brothers, Dorothy Divack, Leslie Divack, Jim Harris, Dana Durst Lawrence, Richard Lawrence, Martha Jane McNally, Patricia O'Neil, Saemi Ladue, and Claudette Jeminez.

my colleagues who encouraged me to the finish line: Jim Frey, Mollie Giles, Jay Schaefer, Sandra Dijkstra, and "Danno."

Julie Rubenstein and Molly Allen, kindred souls who understood and shared my vision of this book.

Special Thanks to:

my mother, Lois Marie Pattillo, M.A., Ph.D.
my grandmother, India Anette Peyton
my brother, Conrad Pattillo
my daughter, Kelli Beals
my nephews, Barry and Conrad Pattillo

Introduction

During the 1950s, most of the United States was **segregated**. African Americans did not have the same freedoms as white Americans. They were treated as if they were not as important as white people. African Americans had to go to separate schools, churches, and restaurants. They could not use the same restrooms, water fountains, and buses that white people used. Many African American schools had inferior books and equipment. The Supreme Court supported these divisions, calling them "separate but equal." But things were not equal.

In 1954, a case called *Brown* v. *The Board of Education of Topeka* went before the Supreme Court. Linda Brown was an eight-year-old African American girl who lived in Topeka, Kansas. She lived a few blocks from a public school for white students. But she had to walk more than a mile to an African American school. Her parents applied for her to go to a school attended by mostly white children, but she was not allowed because she was African American.

Key Concepts

segregrated *adj.* separated into groups by race

11

The Browns sued the Topeka school board and argued that segregated schools were unfair. On May 17, 1954, the Supreme Court ruled that segregated schools were unconstitutional.

This historic court decision outlawed segregation in schools. But it also implied that all forms of segregation were unconstitutional. This belief inspired the civil rights movement, which challenged all segregation.

Martin Luther King, Jr., was an important civil rights leader. King believed in using nonviolent **protest** to bring about change. He believed that there was no **dignity** in violence. Perhaps the most famous civil rights protest took place in 1963. President Kennedy had proposed the Civil Rights Act to make segregation illegal. King led more than 200,000 people in a march through Washington, D.C., to support the bill. The march ended with his famous "I Have a Dream" speech. The bill was signed into law in 1964.

Melba Pattillo Beals grew up during these civil rights struggles. She was twelve years old when *Brown* v. *The Board of Education* was decided. That ruling changed her life. Segregated schools all around the country were forced to **integrate**. She was one of nine African American students chosen to integrate an all-white high school in Little Rock, Arkansas.

Warriors Don't Cry is Melba's account of her year at Central High School. It is the true story of a courageous teenager who endured **hatred**, threats, and acts of violence. Her story gives readers a personal look at these historical events and reminds us to never take our freedoms for granted.

Key Concepts

protest *n.* organized public action objecting to a law or policy

dignity *n.* respect

integrate *v.* to combine; to join together; to mix

hatred *n.* extreme dislike; hostility

Rosa Parks's Boycott

In Montgomery, Alabama in 1955, African Americans were required to sit in the backseats of buses. On December 1, Rosa Parks, a 42-year-old African American woman, took a seat in the front when no seats in back were available. She was ordered to give her seat to a white passenger. She refused to move and was arrested.

The Montgomery Bus Boycott was organized by the African American community to protest segregated buses. African Americans refused to ride the buses until the unfair laws were changed. Martin Luther King, Jr., led this nonviolent protest. In November of 1956, the Supreme Court declared segregation on public buses unconstitutional.

From the Author

Some people call me a heroine because I was one of nine black teenagers who integrated Central High School in Little Rock, Arkansas, in 1957. At the age of fifteen I faced angry mobs violent enough to compel President Eisenhower to send combat-ready 101st Airborne soldiers to quell the violence. I endured a year of school days filled with events unlike any others in the history of this country. Although this happened over thirty-five years ago, I remember being inside Central High School as though it were yesterday.

From the beginning I kept a diary, and my mother, Dr. Lois Pattillo, a high school English teacher, kept copious notes and clipped a sea of newspaper articles. I began the first draft of this book when I was eighteen, but in the ensuing years, I could not face the ghosts that its pages called up. Now enough time has elapsed to allow healing to take place, enabling me to tell my story without bitterness.

In some instances I have changed people's names to protect their identities. But all the incidents recounted here are based on the diary I kept, on news clippings, and on the recollections of my family and myself. While some of the conversations have been re-created, the story is accurate and conveys my truth of what it was like to live in the midst of a civil rights firestorm.

1

My grandmother ~~India~~ always said God had **pointed a finger at** our family, asking for just a bit more discipline, more praying, and more hard work because he had blessed us with good health and good brains. My mother was one of the first few blacks to integrate the University of Arkansas, graduating in 1954. Three years later, when Grandma discovered I would be one of the first blacks to attend Central High School, she said the nightmare that had surrounded my birth **was proof positive** that destiny had assigned me a special task.

First off, I was born on Pearl Harbor Day, December 7, 1941. Mother says while she was giving birth to me, there was a big uproar, with the announcement that the Japanese had bombed Pearl Harbor. She remembers how astonished she was, and yet her focus was necessarily on **the task at hand**. There was trouble with my delivery because Mom was tiny and I was nine pounds. The doctor used **forceps** to deliver me and injured my scalp. A few days later, I fell ill with a massive infection. Mother took me to the white hospital, which reluctantly treated the families of black men who worked on the railroad. A doctor

....

pointed a finger at chosen
was proof positive proved, showed
the task at hand my birth
forceps a tool that grabbed my head

1. What was Melba's Mom's job?

2. What type of neighberhood did she live in?

17

operated to save my life by inserting a drainage system beneath my scalp.

Twenty-four hours later I wasn't getting better. Whenever Mother sought help, neither nurses nor doctors would take her seriously enough to examine me. Instead, they said, "Just give it time."

Two days after my operation, my temperature soared to 106 and I started **convulsing**. Mother sent for the minister to **give me the last rites**, and relatives were gathering to say farewell.

That evening, while Grandmother sat in my hospital room, rocking me back and forth as she hummed her favorite hymn, "On the Battlefield for My Lord," Mother paced the floor weeping aloud in her despair. A black janitor who was sweeping the hallway asked why she was crying. She explained that I was dying because the infection in my head had grown worse.

The man extended his sympathy. As he turned to walk away, dragging his broom behind him, he mumbled that he guessed the Epsom salts hadn't worked after all. Mother ran after him asking what he meant. He explained that a couple of days before, he had been cleaning the operating room as they finished up with my surgery. He had heard the doctor tell the white nurse to irrigate my head with Epsom salts and warm water every two or three hours or I wouldn't make it.

Mother shouted the words "Epsom salts and water" as she raced down the hall, desperately searching for a nurse. The woman was indignant, saying, yes, come to think of it, the doctor had said something about Epsom salts. "But we don't

....

convulsing shaking violently; having seizures
give me the last rites pray over me before I died

coddle niggers," she growled.

Mother didn't **talk back to** the nurse. She knew Daddy's job **was at stake**. Instead, she sent for Epsom salts and began the treatment right away. Within two days, I was remarkably better. The minister went home, and the sisters from the church abandoned their death watch, declaring they had witnessed a miracle.

So fifteen years later, when I was selected to integrate Central High, Grandmother said, "Now you see, that's the reason God spared your life. You're supposed to **carry this banner for** our people."

Black folks aren't born expecting segregation, prepared from day one to follow its confining rules. Nobody presents you with a handbook when you're teething and says, "Here's how you must behave as a second-class citizen." Instead, the humiliating expectations and traditions of segregation creep over you, slowly stealing a teaspoonful of your self-esteem each day.

By the time I was four years old, I was asking questions neither my mother nor grandmother cared to answer. "Why do the white people write 'Colored' on all the ugly drinking fountains, the dingy restrooms, and the back of the buses? When will we get our turn to be in charge?" Grandma India would only say, "In God's time. Be patient, child, and tell God all about it."

I remember sitting on the dining room floor, writing letters to God in my Indian Head tablet. I painstakingly formed the alphabet just as Grandma had taught me to do in order to

----

coddle niggers give special treatment to African Americans
talk back to argue with
was at stake could be taken away
carry this banner for be a leader to

distract me from my asthma cough. I could do the multiplication table through ten and read and write simple sentences by the age of four as a result of all those long nights working with her.

When I was five, I had my first true **bout with testing the harsh realities of segregation**. My family—Grandmother, Mother, Daddy, and my brother, Conrad, plus most of my aunts and uncles—had gathered at Fair Park for a Fourth of July picnic. As usual we were separated from the white people, set apart in a wooded section away from the pool and the merry-go-round. While the grownups busied themselves setting up the meal I made my escape, sneaking away to ride the merry-go-round. I **had had my eye on** one horse in particular, Prancer, the one I had dreamed about during all those months as I saved up the five pennies I needed to ride him.

I reached up to give the **concessionaire** my money. "There's no space for you here," the man said. But I pointed to Prancer's empty saddle. That's when he shouted at me and banged hard on the counter, spilling my coins on the ground. "You don't belong here, **picaninny**." I didn't know what that word meant. But his growling voice hurt my ears and made my knees shake. Angry faces glared at me as though I'd done something terribly wrong. Scurrying past the people waiting in line, I was so terrified that I didn't even take the time to pick up my precious pennies. At five I learned that there was to be no space for me on that merry-go-round no matter how many saddles stood empty.

As a young child, my life was centered around the big,

....

**bout with testing the harsh realities of
segregation** experience with racism
had had my eye on wanted to ride
concessionaire person who was selling the tickets
picaninny little African American girl

old, white wood-frame house at 1121 Cross Street that was my home. I lived there with my mother, Lois; her mother, my grandmother India; my father, Howell; and my brother, Conrad. Seven red cement stairs led up to the front door. A giant rubber plant stood just inside the front hallway next to tall **mahogany** bookcases that held the cherished volumes of Shakespeare, Chaucer, and Emily Dickinson, and of James Welden Johnson and Langston Hughes that Grandma and Mother loved so much. Some of the shelves held the textbooks Mother used for teaching seventh-grade English and for the night classes she took to get her **master's degree**.

Next came the living room with its **tattered**, overstuffed green velvet chair and matching couch. The half-moon-shaped radio with brass knobs sat on a round mahogany table. Wine-colored leather chairs stood on either side. Great-grandma Ripley's clock and a copper horse that had belonged to Great-grandpa rested on the mantel over the fireplace.

The kitchen had a huge old-fashioned stove, a red chrome-trimmed breakfast table and chairs, bright yellow walls, and a linoleum floor with visible marks of **wear and tear**. Grandma could usually be found scrubbing it sparkling clean or baking cornbread, simmering collard greens, or preparing her special gourmet salmon soufflé. She had learned to cook some of her fancy dishes when she worked as a maid in white ladies' kitchens on Park Hill.

For as long as I can remember, I spent late afternoons with Grandma India in her garden, tending her four o'clock plants.

....

mahogany dark-colored wood
master's degree advanced college degree
tattered torn; worn out
wear and tear being old; heavy use

I would stand beside her holding on to her skirt as she pulled the weeds or held the water hose. That's when we had our private talks. Once when I was six or so, I explained to her that I believed each human being was really only a spirit—made by God, and that our bodies were like clothes hanging in the closet. I said I thought that one day I would be able to exchange my body for a white body, and then I could be in charge.

(RP)

"Some of your thinking is right, child. We are not these bodies, we are spirits, God's ideas. But you must **strive** to be the best of what God made you. You don't want to be white, what you really want is to be free, and freedom is **a state of mind**."

wishes
she
was
white

"Yes, ma'am, but . . ."

"I hope you haven't told anyone else about spirits and bodies." She squeezed my hand. "Well, have you?"

"No, ma'am."

"Good. It's time you started **keeping a diary** so's you can write down these thoughts and share them with me sometimes, but mostly keep them to yourself and tell God."

The next time she went to town she brought me a pink diary that I could lock with a little key. Most evenings before sleeping, I looked forward to going to my bedroom to write to God.

My room was a place for my stuffed animals to live and a home for my huge brown Raggedy Ann doll, the one Grandma India made for me. It was a magical place where I **daydreamed** for hours as I listened to music or radio shows. There I could be whoever I wanted; I could be white—I could be free.

My brother, Conrad's, bedroom was filled with strange

....

strive work very hard

a state of mind a way of thinking and acting

keeping a diary writing in a personal book

daydreamed made up stories in my head

22

trucks, glass jars of crawly bugs, and a wooden train Daddy made for him. Conrad spent lots of time counting marbles, putting puzzles together, and playing **Monopoly**. His room always seemed to be cluttered with pieces and parts of things, and Daddy would often march into Conrad's room and demand that he put all his toys and trucks back into the red wooden box they had built together.

Daddy worked for the Missouri Pacific Railroad as a hostler's helper. He would arrive home, his huge muscular body obviously tired from the physical labor of his job. Mother constantly reminded him that if he'd finish just one more course, he could graduate from college and have a professional job that paid more. But he resisted, saying he preferred to work outside in the fresh air, where he was free. He loved hunting and fishing and getting away to the wilds where nobody could bother him. It made Mother very angry that he wouldn't follow her advice. I worried they might do what my friend Carolyn's parents did—get a divorce.

The dining room with its big oval table was the place we gathered each night for dinner and evening games. Daddy sat in the brown leather chair, reading his newspaper and working his crossword puzzles. Grandma entertained us with reading or checkers and chess so we wouldn't bother Mother as she studied for her night-school exams. She was determined to complete her master's degree.

....

Monopoly board games

With the passage of time, I became increasingly aware of how all of the adults around me were living with constant fear and apprehension. It felt as though we always had **a white foot pressed against the back of our necks**. I was feeling more and more vulnerable as I watched them continually struggle to solve the mystery of what white folks expected of them. They behaved as though it were an awful sin to overlook even one of those unspoken rules and **step out of "their place,"** to cross some invisible line. And yet lots of discussions in my household were about how to cross that line, when to cross that line, and who could cross that invisible line without getting hurt.

There were so many times when I felt shame, and all the hope drained from my soul as I watched the adults in my family **kowtow to** white people. Whenever we shopped at the grocery store, they behaved as though they were worried about something.

The grocer, tall, skinny Mr. Waylan, with his Adam's apple sticking out above his collar, his fish-belly blue-white skin and oversized fingernails, was the white man I saw most often. At least twice a week, I would accompany one or more of the adults in my family to his store.

Mr. Waylan's store was one of my favorite places because going there was sometimes like going to a neighborhood party. Mostly our people shopped there, although a few whites from a nearby neighborhood came there, too. There was sawdust on the floor, and the air was filled with the aroma of spices, fruits, onions, nuts, and potatoes. Maybe it was the festive colors and

----

a white foot pressed against the back of our necks white people telling us what we could not do

step out of "their place" do something the white people told them they were not allowed to do

kowtow to be afraid of and obey the rules of

sounds that reminded me of a party.

Early one Friday evening, when the store was crowded, our entire family went in for a shopping spree. We had Mama's teaching check, Daddy's railroad check, and the money Grandma India had earned from her work as a maid. It was one of those times when we all felt joy and peace and lots of hope. I looked forward to the bill paying because the grocer sometimes rewarded Conrad and me with Sugar Daddy suckers after the grown-ups handed over the money.

Grandma was the first to look over Mr. Waylan's bill. Her forehead wrinkled; she mumbled and handed it to Daddy. He looked it over. By the time Mother examined the bill, all their faces were **grim**. They quickly moved Conrad and me with them to a corner of the store.

They were certain the bill overcharged them by twenty-two dollars. That was more than a day's pay, Daddy said. Still, they seemed frightened to **speak up**. After lots of whispered angry words, they decided to complain. Although Grandma approached the grocer in a calm, respectful way, he shouted back at her in an angry voice—loud enough for everyone within a block to hear. He said he **gave us credit** when we didn't have eating money, so he expected us to pay without complaining.

Seeing Daddy's jaw tighten and his eyes narrow, Grandma touched his hand to **stay him**. There was an ominous silence in the store. Everybody was staring at us. Other people in the store, some of them our friends, stood absolutely still, fear in their eyes.

....

grim unhappy
speak up tell the grocer the bill was wrong
gave us credit let us take food and pay later
stay him keep him quiet

At first Mother, Grandma, and Daddy stood paralyzed. Then Mother took a deep breath, stepped forward, and said in a commanding voice, "Even when we're being overcharged?"

"You just watch your mouth or you'all will be eating beans next month." The grocer was shaking his fist at Mother Lois. There was fire in Daddy's eyes, but once again Grandma looked at him and he backed down; the three of them cowered like children before a chastising parent. There was a long moment 4-H of complete silence. All at once Grandma started to pull dollars out of her purse and Daddy did the same. Together, they paid the full amount.

Mama quickly shoved Conrad and me out the door. We'd **make do with** what was in our cupboards for the next few days, Daddy said. We wouldn't be going to that store anymore.

On the way home Grandma **fussed and fumed**, saying she was **fed up with** buying day-old bread and slightly rotting meat for one and a half times the price fresh food was sold to white folks. I couldn't stop wondering why Mama, Grandma, and Daddy couldn't talk back to that white man.

Daddy was a tall man, over six feet four, with broad shoulders and big muscles in his arms. He could toss me in the air and catch me or hoist me over the fence with ease. Until that moment, I had thought he could **take on the world**, if he had to protect me. But watching him kowtow to the grocer made me know it wasn't so. It frightened me and made me think a lot about how, if I got into trouble with white people, the folks I counted on most in my life for protection couldn't help me

....

make do with eat
fussed and fumed complained angrily
fed up with tired of
take on the world do anything

at all. I was beginning to **resign myself to** the fact that white people were definitely in charge, and there was nothing we could do about it. RP

The next day Grandma called all her friends and tried to get them to agree to form a group to shop across town. All but one person warned her not to cause trouble. After she had dialed at least ten numbers, she sank down into her chair and sat silent for a long while. Then she picked up her Bible and read aloud the verse that cleared away the tears in her eyes: "And Ethiopia shall stretch forth her wings." With a smile on her face and fire in her eyes she said, "Be patient, our people's turn will come. You'll see. Your lifetime will be different from mine. I might not live to see the changes, but you will. . . . Oh, yes, my child, you will."

But as time passed without **significant** changes in my life, I was becoming **increasingly anxious** waiting for Ethiopia to stretch forth her wings. In my diary I wrote:

What if Grandma is wrong?—what if God can't fix things. What if the white people are always gonna be in charge. God, now, please give me some sign you are there and you are gonna do something to change my life. Please hurry!
—Melba Pattillo, age eight,
a Sunday school student

....

resign myself to accept, understand

significant important, major

increasingly anxious more worried

BEFORE YOU MOVE ON...

1. **Summarize** Reread page 20. What was Melba's first experience with segregation? How did it make her feel?

2. **Sequence** Reread pages 24–26. Melba's family went to Mr. Waylan's store to shop. What happened next?

LOOK AHEAD Read pages 28–40 to find out how seriously racism affected Melba.

2

How could I ever forget May 17, 1954, the day the Supreme Court ruled in *Brown* v. *Board of Education of Topeka, Kansas*, that separate public schools for whites and blacks were illegal? The adults around me behaved so strangely that their images became **a freeze-frame, forever preserved** in my mind. I learned lessons on that day that I will remember for the rest of my life.

I was twelve years old. That afternoon, I sat at my desk in my seventh-grade class at Dunbar Junior High, copying from the blackboard. My teacher had been called outside. When she returned, she **appeared** frightened and nervous. Erasing the blackboard before we could finish our copying, she spoke breathlessly about *Brown* v. *Board of Education.*

"Does that mean we have to go to school with white people?" my friend Carl asked as **a chorus of voices echoed** his question.

"Yes, maybe. But you needn't concern yourself with that. Collect your things. You'all **are dismissed** early today." Although she said the Brown case was something we should

....

a freeze-frame, forever preserved like a photograph

appeared seemed

a chorus of voices echoed other students repeated

are dismissed can leave school

be proud of, something to celebrate, her face didn't look at all happy. I didn't understand why she was in such a big rush to dismiss us that way, but I didn't ask. Going home to be with my grandmother India was something I looked forward to every day. Peering over the book or newspaper she was reading, she would always greet me the same way: "And what did you learn today?" She hadn't finished high school, but she had read lots of books, and she studied everything and everybody all the time. Over an after-school snack of warm gingerbread and milk, the two of us would talk and laugh until it was time for me to start my chores—and homework.

Now as we left school I heard my teacher's **quivering** voice: "Pay attention to where you're walking. Walk in groups, don't walk alone." She stood at the top of the steps, telling us to hurry.

Once outside, I realized I had forgotten a math book, but when I tried to get it, she blocked my way, telling me that I should go on with the others. I couldn't imagine why she **was so insistent that I** hurry home. She even said she would excuse my homework assignment the next day. She had never excused undone homework for any reason before.

I **trailed** behind the others as I **pondered** her strange behavior. I paid little attention to where I was going. It was, after all, a familiar route, one I had walked since age six. I usually took a shortcut across a vacant block, through a grassy field filled with persimmon trees. In spring, ripened fruit littered the ground to make walking a hazardous, slippery adventure.

Sometimes it wasn't always safe to take that shortcut because

....

quivering shaking, nervous
was so insistent that I ordered me to
trailed walked slowly
pondered thought about

of Marissa. She was an older girl who frightened us. She would suddenly become very mean, striking out for no reason. I would be walking along that path, and all at once I'd be attacked by a shower of overripe persimmons. There was no way I could protect myself or fight back because Marissa was so big and overpowering. At twelve, I was considered tall for my age; most folks thought I was fifteen. But Marissa was even bigger. Nobody knew how old she was—we thought she was about sixteen—much too old to be in our class.

Marissa was different; the teachers called her "retarded." Even though she often misbehaved, adults never did anything about it, maybe because her father was a rich minister in our community. As I crossed the field, I knew that I risked having Marissa rush out of the bushes at any moment. But I also knew I could get past her if I gave her my lunch apple or my allowance money. Otherwise, I felt I was pretty safe in that field—safe enough to lapse into my daydreams. This was my special time of the day—when I could sing as loud as I wanted and make up new daydreams about being a movie star or moving North to New York or out West to California.

I didn't agree with the radio announcers who described Little Rock as a nice, clean Southern town, a place where my people and whites got along peacefully. City officials **boasted** there hadn't been a **Klan hanging of one of our people** in at least ten years.

The city fathers bragged about the way our people and white folks were working **"side by side."** Of the 107,300 Little Rock

....

boasted bragged that

Klan hanging of one of our people murder of an African American by a group of racist white people

"side by side" together

citizens, blacks numbered about 30,000. They said blacks earned good wages, but that wasn't true. Most of my people who earned tolerable salaries were either teachers, preachers, or doctors. For us, there were very few jobs as clerks, policemen, bus drivers, or insurance salesmen.

My mother had long ago grown weary of trying to get Daddy to finish up his university courses. In fact, she had given up on him by the time I was seven. That's when they divorced. Even though he had been gone from the house almost five years, I still missed him, most often at dinnertime and on those evenings when we gathered in the dining room for family games. It made Conrad and me sad not to have him there. Often on those walks home from school, I daydreamed that we were a family again—that Daddy finished school to make Mother happy and she canceled the divorce to let him come back home.

As I entered the persimmon field, I sank deep into my thoughts, but a few steps past the big tree at the front of the path, I heard a rustling sound. I stood perfectly still, looking all around. I didn't see **a soul**. Suddenly, as I came near to the end of the field, a man's **gravel voice snatched me from the secret place in my head**.

"You want a ride, girl?" He didn't sound at all like anybody I knew. There it was again, that stranger's voice calling out to me. "Want a ride?"

"Who is it?" I asked, **barely able to squeeze the words out**.

"I got candy in the car. Lots of candy." I crept forward, and then I saw him—a big white man, even taller than my father,

....

a soul anyone

gravel voice snatched me from the secret place in my head deep voice scared me

barely able to squeeze the words out frightened

broad and huge, like a wrestler. He was coming toward me fast. I turned **on my heels and fled** in the opposite direction, back the way I had come.

"You better come on and take a ride home. You hear me, girl?"

"No, sir," I yelled, "no thank you." But he kept coming. My heart was racing almost as fast as my feet. I couldn't hear anything except for the sound of my saddle shoes pounding the ground and the thud of his feet close behind me. That's when he started talking about "niggers" wanting to go to school with his children and how he wasn't going to **stand for it**. My cries for help drowned out the sound of his words, but he laughed and said it was no use because nobody would hear me.

I was running as fast as I could. The lace on my shoe came untied. My feet got tangled. As I hit the ground, I bit down hard on my tongue. I felt his strong hands clutch my back. I **bolted** up, struggling to get away. He pulled me down and turned me on my back. I looked up into his face, looming close above me like the monster on a movie screen. I struggled against him, but he was too strong.

He slapped me hard across the face. I covered my eyes with my hands and waited for him to strike me again. Instead, I felt him squirm against me, and then I saw him taking his pants down. In my house, private parts were always kept private. I couldn't figure out what he was doing, but I knew it had to be bad. I scratched and kicked and thrashed against him with every ounce of strength I **could muster**. His huge fist smashed hard

....

on my heels and fled quickly and ran
stand for it let that happen
bolted stood up quickly
could muster had in my body

against my face. I struggled to push him back and to **keep the dark curtain of unconsciousness from descending over me**.

"I'll show you niggers the Supreme Court can't run my life," he said as his hand ripped at my underpants. A voice inside my head told me I was going to die, that there was nothing I could do about it. White men were in charge. But then I could hear Grandma India saying over and over again, "God is always with you." I fought to keep my underpants and to roll the man off of me.

All at once, he frowned and let out an awful moan, and grabbed for the back of his head. It was Marissa banging on his head with her leather book bag. "Melba . . . Melba, . . . run," she shouted. When he rolled off me, I scrambled free.

Marissa shouted to me to run faster. She let go of her book bag and dragged me by my arm. If we didn't hurry, we'd get **raped**, she said over and over. Raped? What's raped? I asked as we scurried across the field and back into the street. We raced up the middle of the street, not stopping to talk to anybody, not even the people we knew who tried to say hello. Breathless and shaken, we finally reached my backyard.

My brother, Conrad, braked his bicycle to question me. What was the matter with my face? Why were my clothes torn? I felt ashamed as I wondered if he and his playmate Clark could guess that a strange man had touched me. Just then Grandma India opened the back door. As soon as she looked at me she frowned and sent Conrad and Clark away.

Marissa explained what had happened to us, and she repeated

....

keep the dark curtain of unconsciousness from descending over me stay alert

raped sexually attacked

the word "rape." "But he didn't do it all the way," she said. By then I had figured out it was something awful and dirty. Before I could ask Grandma more about it, she put a cold cloth to my face and rushed me into the bathtub.

"Now you soak a while, child. When the water goes down the drain, it will take away all that white man's evil with it." She had a **curious** look on her face, one I'd never seen before. Then she said something that made me realize just how, awful things really were. "We'll burn the clothes you took off. I got your fresh clothing on a stool, just outside the door."

I couldn't believe my ears! **"Waste not, want not"** had always been her rule. What had happened must have been truly disgusting to make her destroy my good clothing. I sat in silence wondering if I could ever **redeem myself** in the eyes of the Lord.

Later, I heard Grandma talking to my father on the telephone as Mother Lois came in the back door with her usual cheerful greetings. I didn't climb out of the tub. Instead I scrubbed myself in those hot suds to wash away my **shame**. When Grandma came to check on me, she must have seen the distress in my expression, because she promised the Lord would still count me as one of his good girls because I hadn't done anything wrong.

I listened for so long while the grown-ups argued in loud whispers about calling the police that my bath water turned cold. As I climbed out of the tub and got dressed, I heard Daddy's voice. When I walked into the kitchen, for the first

....

curious strange
"Waste not, want not" Never throw away anything useful
redeem myself be good again
shame embarrassment; bad feelings

time ever I saw tears in my father's eyes. As he reached to hug me, he said, "We ain't gonna call the law. Those white police **are liable to** do something worse to her than what already happened."

Grandma told me not to talk about what had happened with anyone, especially not Conrad. She said I had to pray for that evil white man, pray every day for twenty-one days, asking God to forgive him and **teach him right**. That way, she promised I'd get over the feelings of shame.

I wore my knees out praying night after night—I even got up early to get in extra prayers. Grandma was right. By the time my bruises went away, I didn't feel ashamed anymore.

In my diary I wrote:

> *It's important for me to read the newspaper, every single day God sends, even if I have to spend my own nickel to buy it. I have to keep up with what the men on the Supreme Court are doing. That way I can stay home on the day the justices vote decisions that make white men want to rape me.*

The daily papers were full of news about the *Brown* v. *Board of Education* case. Little Rock's white people were saying the same things as the "raping" man had said. I couldn't imagine they would ever change their minds and allow their children to go to school with me, no matter what laws those men on the Supreme Court made. But on May 24, 1955, the newspapers said the Little Rock school board had **adopted a plan to limit integration** to

....

are liable to will probably; might
teach him right teach him to be a good person
adopted a plan to limit integration decided to allow African Americans to go only

Central High School. They weren't going to allow it to actually begin, however, for two years—not till September, 1957.

When my teacher asked if anyone who lived within the Central High School district wanted to attend school with white people, I raised my hand. As I signed my name on the paper they passed around, I thought about all those times I'd gone past Central High, wanting to see inside. I was certain it would take a miracle to integrate Little Rock's schools. But I reasoned that if schools were open to my people, I would also **get access to other opportunities I had been denied**, like going to shows at Robinson Auditorium, or sitting on the first floor of the movie theater.

By December 1, 1955, I began to realize that Grandma was right. Our people were **stretching out to knock down the fences of** segregation. I read in the newspaper that one of our people, a woman named Rosa Parks, had refused to give up her seat to a white man on an Alabama bus. Her willingness *E* to be arrested rather than give in one more time led to the Montgomery, Alabama, bus boycott. I felt such a surge of pride when I thought about how my people had banded together to force a change. It gave me hope that maybe things in Little Rock could change.

On February 8, 1956, the NAACP filed suit in Federal District Court to make the schools integrate immediately. Referring to a poll that said 85 percent of all Arkansas's people opposed integration, Governor Orval Faubus announced his refusal to support the integration of our state's schools.

....

get access to other opportunities I had been denied be able to do things I had not been able to do

stretching out to knock down the fences of trying to stop *ᴥ ᴥ ᴥ*

In early August of 1957, Johnny Mathis had his first big song, "Chances Are," on the **hit parade**. That month a Mrs. Clyde Thomason, secretary of a new group called the League of Central High Mothers, **filed a petition for an injunction** to keep the Little Rock school board from carrying out its gradual integration plan.

About that time, I decided to quit worrying about whether I should tell my parents I had signed up to go to Central. After all, if white mothers were fighting integration, it had little chance of success. I knew very well the power of my own mother and grandmother. Besides, I needed all my mind's space for living my daydreams, since Conrad, Mother, Grandma, and I were about to go North. We were driving to Cincinnati, Ohio, to visit my great-uncle Clancey, on mother's side of the family. He was an Episcopalian priest, and his wife, Julie, was a music teacher.

For me, Cincinnati was **the promised land**. After a few days there, I lost that Little Rock feeling of being choked and kept in "my place" by white people. I felt free, as though I could soar above the clouds. I was both frightened and excited when the white neighbors who lived across the street invited me for dinner. It was the first time white people had ever wanted to eat with me or talk to me about ordinary things. Over the dinner table, I found out they were people just like me. They used the same blue linen dinner napkins that Grandma India favored.

....

hit parade radio
filed a petition for an injunction legally tried
the promised land a wonderful place without segregation

They treated me like I was an equal, like I belonged with them.

Afterward we went to a drive-in movie. The neighbor's daughter, Cindy, who was exactly my age, stood beside me as I walked right up to the concession stand to buy popcorn. No one even looked at me with evil eyes or called me a name! Still, my heart was pounding and my palms were wet as I squeezed through that big crowd of white people to get back to the car.

Right in the middle of downtown Cincinnati, we walked with our heads held high, acting as proud as could be. Neither Mother nor Grandmother ever once stepped aside to let a white person pass. Sometimes we **held our ground** and white people walked around us. We sauntered through all the big department stores, touching expensive things without the white clerks **giving us a second look**. I even used the rest room, and the white ladies smiled and said hello. Later, as I sat at the lunch counter in the **five-and-dime** to have a root beer, I could hardly eat **for keeping watch** all around me. But no white person so much as frowned at me. That evening Uncle Clancey took us to a fancy restaurant where white waiters smiled and bowed, and asked if I wanted anything.

"Melba will be hard to get along with after all this spoiled treatment," Mama said as we ate, laughed, and talked. I'd never had lobster or cottage fries before, or had a white man play the piano just to make my meal go down easy.

It was mid-August and we'd been in paradise for more than a week. I was wondering how I could tell Mama I wasn't ever going back to Little Rock. I planned to beg and plead with

....

held our ground did not move out of the way

giving us a second look thinking we were going to steal

five-and-dime local store

for keeping watch because I could not stop looking

Uncle Clancey to let me live with them and finish high school in Cincinnati. I thought I had a pretty good chance of having things go my way until one evening when we sat watching the national news.

"That was your father on the phone." Mother appeared to be annoyed as she spoke. "He said to pay close attention to the news because he got a call today saying Melba's been assigned to go to Central High with the white people."

All ears perked up when the announcer started talking about Little Rock. He said seventeen children from my community had been selected to enter the all-white Central High School in the 1957 fall term.

Grandma stood and walked over to the television set, signaling us to be silent. The announcer talked about **Thurgood Marshall** and the NAACP asking the Federal District Court to start integration immediately. A judge had agreed and issued an order preventing Mrs. Thomason and her mothers' group from interfering.

We all stood like statues as the newsman talked about Little Rock's segregationists, who were determined to stop our children from entering white schools **at any cost**. I couldn't make myself stand still; an awful fear vibrated through my body.

Conrad asked if he could go, too. Grandma India said an emphatic "No." By then Mother was pale, her lips drawn tight as she glared at me. All of them circled around me. With horrified expressions, they looked at me as though I had lied or sassed Grandma or grown a second nose. I stood in the middle

....

All ears perked up We all listened closely
Thurgood Marshall a famous African American lawyer
at any cost no matter what they had to do

of the room, hoping the floor would swallow me up as they **grilled** me.

When had I planned on telling them? Why did I sign my name to the paper saying I lived near Central and wanted to go, without asking their permission? Did I consider that my decision might endanger our family? All the while I was trying to back away from their harsh inquisition. I no longer cared the least bit about Little Rock; I just wanted to live right there in Cincinnati. *RP concerns*

It was like a nightmare—suddenly my joy and freedom ended. All night they yelled and paced and discussed. By morning Mama wasn't talking to me. She ate breakfast with a frown on her face. **Grandma's mouth was poked out**, but she talked to me, saying over and over again that I was too smart for my **britches**. *E*

That was the end of my vacation. We hurried home to begin living a life I had never imagined in my wildest dreams. Grandma **called it "all Hades breaking loose."**

....

grilled questioned

Grandma's mouth was poked out Grandma looked angry

britches own good

called it "all Hades breaking loose" said it was like living in Hell

BEFORE YOU MOVE ON...

1. **Cause and Effect** What caused the stranger to attack Melba?

2. **Conclusions** Reread pages 39–40. What can you conclude about Melba's decision to attend a white school?

LOOK AHEAD Read pages 41–50 to find out if the governor supported integration.

3

By the time we arrived home from Cincinnati, my life was already **upside down**. I was living with one **concern**—preparing to take part in the integration of Central High School. It consumed much of the time and energy of my entire family. I could see it was consuming the energy of the entire city. Nobody I spoke with or watched on local television or heard on the radio talked of anything else.

I was drowning in unfamiliar activities and sounds—the sound of the constantly ringing telephone, of people talking loud in my ear and expressing their views about integration, of reporters' urgent voices describing what integration might do to the city and the South, and of official-looking adults **lecturing** me about integration for hours in **closed** meetings.

Meetings—my life was filled with meetings, boring meetings with the white superintendent of schools, the school board, with Central High School officials, with NAACP officials. For the first time, I met Mrs. Daisy Bates, a petite and smartly dressed, steely-eyed woman who was the Arkansas state president of the NAACP. She seemed very calm and brave considering the

---

upside down completely different; changed
concern worry, problem
lecturing talking to; teaching
closed private

caravans of segregationists said to be driving past her house and tossing firebombs and rocks through her windows. They saw her as their enemy not only because of her position but because she and her husband owned the *Arkansas State Press*, a newspaper that was the **sole voice** for our community.

The only good thing about the meetings was that they allowed me to visit with my friends—the other students who would be integrating Central. I had known most of them all my life. At one point there had been sixteen others, but some of them chose not to participate because of the threats of violence. It frightened me to see our number **dwindling**. Still, I was delighted with those I knew were definitely going.

In the end, there were nine of us. Ernest Green, the oldest and a senior, was a member of my church. His warm eyes and quick smile greeted me each week at Sunday school. His aunt, Mrs. Gravely, had taught me history in junior high.

Tall, thin Terrence Roberts was a junior like me, and a friend since first grade. He was a very verbal person who could be counted on to give the funniest, most intelligent analysis of any situation. I adored his way of always humming a cheerful tune when he wasn't talking.

Jefferson Thomas was a quiet, soft-spoken athlete—tops in his class. His sense of humor was subtle, the kind that makes you giggle aloud when you're not supposed to.

Elizabeth Eckford was petite, a very quiet, private person who had smiled and waved at me across the hallway at our old school. She was **regal in her bearing** and, like all of us, very

----

caravans large numbers; groups
sole voice only newspaper
dwindling becoming smaller and smaller
regal in her bearing proud and smart

serious about her studies.

Thelma Mothershed and I were friends who saw each other frequently. Small like Elizabeth but with a very pale complexion, her wise eyes peered through thick-lensed horn-rimmed glasses. She had a heart problem that at times changed her **pallor** to a purplish hue and forced her to rest on her haunches to **catch her breath**.

Best of all, my special friend Minnijean Brown was going. Since she lived only a block away from me, we saw each other almost every day. We had much in common; both of us were tall for our age, and we shared daydreams—our worship of Johnny Mathis and Nat Cole, and our desire to sing.

Carlotta Walls was an athlete, very sleek and wonderfully energetic. Everything she said or did was quickly executed. She was a girl-next-door type, always in a good mood, always ready to try something new.

Gloria Ray was another member of my Sunday school class. Delicate in stature, she was as **meticulous** about her attire as she was about her studies. Her all-knowing eyes grew even more intense as she spoke in **softly measured words**.

We integrating students shared many things in common. All of our parents were strict, no-nonsense types. Several of them were teachers and preachers, or held well-established positions in other professions. All our folks were hardworking people who had struggled to own their homes, to provide a stable life for their families. We shared many of the same family values traditional to all small-town Americans.

....

pallor color
catch her breath be able to breathe
meticulous neat and careful
softly measured words a quiet and intelligent voice

Our parents demanded that we behave appropriately at home and in public. I couldn't imagine that any one of us would ever talk back to our folks or other adults. All of us were churchgoing; all our parents demanded good grades in school. Although none of us had a lot of money, we had pride in our appearance. Most of all, we were **individualists** with strong opinions. Each of us planned to go to college.

I felt comfortable being with them, because they were the kind of people my mother allowed me to **associate** with. And after a period of being together so much, I began to feel as though we had formed some kind of group—an odd family of people with one goal: to get inside Central High and stay there for the school year.

On Monday, September 2, Labor Day, our family gathered at Auntie Mae's house for the last picnic of the summer. She was mother's sister, a wonderfully round, cuddly woman with flowing wavy hair and a warm smile. A real **live wire**, she liked to play pranks on people and tell the kind of naughty jokes that made Mother blush and cover my ears.

Her laughter and upbeat attitude always cheered me up. People said I had some of her feisty ways in me. I was certain my auntie Mae could do just about anything. "Rules are made to be broken," she said. "If there's anyone who can integrate that school, it's you. You're just sassy enough to **pull it off**."

"Although I don't know why you'd want to go where you're not wanted," said Uncle Charlie, Mother's brother, puffing

....

individualists independent people
associate be friends; spend time
live wire funny woman
pull it off succeed

on his cigar.

"**To heck with them**," said Auntie Mae. "Besides, I heard a rumor that Governor Faubus is gonna send the National Guard over to the school."

"How do you know that?"

"Mamie Johnson's cousin cooks for that school. They called to tell her where she has to check in tomorrow morning to get past the soldiers." That began a **free-for-all** about integration. It was just what I didn't want to hear. So I drifted off into my daydreams about Vince, the cute boy I liked. I pictured what it might have been like to have him pick me up in his new car at our old school where everybody could see.

Later on that night, Grandma thought we should listen to the governor's speech on television. To our amazement, he announced he had sent troops to Central. And then he said, "They will not act as segregationists or integrationists, but as soldiers called to active duty to carry out their assigned tasks." Then he spoke the words that made chills creep up and down my spine. ". . . But I must state here in all sincerity that it is my opinion, yes, even a conviction, that it will not be possible to **restore or maintain order** and protect the lives and property of the citizens if forcible integration is carried out tomorrow in the schools of this community."

"The governor has finally **flipped his wig**," Mother Lois said, glaring at the moon-faced man on the TV screen.

On the night of the governor's speech, the phone didn't stop ringing. One caller said he knew our address and would be right

....

To heck with them Do not worry about them
free-for-all group discussion
restore or maintain order keep things peaceful
flipped his wig become crazy

over to bomb the house. Grandma went directly to her room, where she took the shotgun she called Mr. Higgenbottom from its leather case in the back of her closet. That night, she set up **her guard post** near the window to the side yard where she thought we were most vulnerable. She sat in her rocking chair beside the antique mahogany end table given her by her mother.

After a moment for **contemplation** and prayer, she stretched her embroidery work tightly over its hoop. With her needles and threads, she settled down for the night with Mr. Higgenbottom across her lap. She sat as erect as those heroic soldiers I'd seen in magazine pictures.

As I tried to fall asleep, I could hear Grandma rocking back and forth in her chair, singing hymns that must have given her the strength to stay alert all night.

That night in my diary I wrote to God:

> *Maybe going to Central High isn't such a good idea after all. It is costing my family a lot of agony and energy, and I haven't even attended one day yet. Will Grandma always have to sit up guarding us. She can't go on sitting there forever. What will become of us. Maybe I should start my plan for moving to Cincinnati. Please give me some sign of what I am to do.*

Late Monday evening the shrill ring of the phone awakened me. Mother took the call from the NAACP telling us not to attend school the next day, Tuesday. We were to wait until we were **notified** before going to Central. Early the next morning

----

her guard post a place to sit and protect the house
contemplation serious thinking
notified called and told it was safe

I caught Grandmother **nodding** at her guard post as I went out to pick up the newspaper. The headlines told the story:

FAUBUS CALLS NATIONAL GUARD
TO KEEP SCHOOL SEGREGATED
Troops Take Over at Central High;
Negroes Told to Wait
—*Arkansas Gazette*, Tuesday, September 3, 1957

Tuesday afternoon, School Superintendent Virgil Blossom **called** a meeting of the nine of us students and our folks. During that meeting, the tall, stocky, grim-faced Blossom breathlessly instructed our parents not to come with us to school the next day. "It will be easier to protect the children if adults aren't there," he said.

The looks on the faces of the adults told me they all were frightened. Not one among them seemed certain of what they were doing.

As we arrived home, the man on the radio explained federal judge Ronald Davies's ruling, ordering integrated classes to begin on Wednesday. The phone **was ringing off the hook**. Our minister said some of the church members were forming a group made up of people from several churches. They would pray and work for peace in the city. At the same time, he said, they would be ready to help us if we needed it.

The call just after midnight from the NAACP didn't really disturb us because we were already receiving a series of late

....

nodding sleeping
called had
was ringing off the hook was constantly ringing

night calls from segregationists who were loud and vulgar in their views. Mrs. Bates said we would meet at Twelfth and Park. The school was between Fourteenth and Sixteenth on Park. Perhaps we would **be accompanied by** several ministers; some of them would be white. She named Reverend Dunbar Ogden, Jr., the white president of the interracial Ministerial Alliance, and two of our ministers, Reverend Z. Z. Driver of the African Methodist Episcopal Church and Reverend Harry Bass of the Methodist Episcopal Church.

JUDGE ORDERS INTEGRATION
—*Arkansas Gazette*, Tuesday, September 3, 1957

Dear Diary,
  It's happening today. What I'm afraid of most is that they won't like me and integration won't work and Little Rock won't become like Cincinnati, Ohio.

By Wednesday morning, September 4, I could hardly believe it was really happening—I was going to Central High School. As I prepared breakfast before leaving home on that first morning, Grandmother India stood over my shoulder watching while I cracked the breakfast eggs for **poaching**.

Every radio in the house was tuned to the stations that gave frequent news reports. **The urgent voices grabbed our attention whether we wanted them to or not.** I'd never heard the news read that often, except when there was a tornado.

....

be accompanied by walk with
poaching cooking
The urgent voices grabbed our attention whether we wanted them to or not. We could not ignore it.

Hundreds of Little Rock citizens are gathered in front of Central High School awaiting the arrival of the Negro children. We're told people have come from as far away as Mississippi, Louisiana, and Georgia to **join forces to halt** integration.

Grandma took my hand as she started the **blessing**, asking the Lord to protect me. I closed my eyes, but not even the breakfast blessing could halt the thoughts buzzing through my mind. As we ate, I hoped no one noticed that I pushed my food about my plate because my stomach didn't want breakfast. Mother spoke my name softly, and I looked up at her. "You don't have to integrate this school. Your grandmother and I will love you, no matter what you decide."

"But I have no choice if we're gonna stay in Little Rock," I said. I couldn't stop hoping that integrating Central High School was the first step to making Little Rock just like Cincinnati, Ohio. Besides, we had been told students of Little Rock's richest and most important white families attended there. They were also probably very smart. As soon as those students got to know us, I **had total faith** they would realize how wrong they had been about our people. RP

"A lot has changed in the two years since you signed up to go to Central. You were younger then," Mother said with a frown on her face. "Maybe it was a **hasty** decision—a decision we'll all regret."

....

join forces to halt work together to stop
blessing prayer
had total faith really believed
hasty bad

Before Mama Lois could say another word, the phone rang. Conrad raced to answer, but Mother was there first. "**Keep your seat**, young man." As she held the phone to her ear, she stood motionless and silent and her face grew **ashen and drawn**. Then she slowly replaced the receiver in its cradle and said, "It's time to go!"

....

Keep your seat Sit down
ashen and drawn pale and tired

BEFORE YOU MOVE ON...

1. **Comparisons** Compare the governor's actions and his speech. What did he think about integration?

2. **Author's Style** Reread pages 46–48. How does the author tell her story?

LOOK AHEAD Read pages 51–66 to find out why Melba ran away from the school.

4

As we walked down the front steps, mother paused and turned to look back at Grandma, who was standing at the edge of the porch. In their glance I saw the fear they had never **voiced** in front of me. Grandma **lingered** for a moment and then rushed to encircle me in her arms once more. "God is always with you," she whispered as she **blinked back tears**.

Trailing behind Mother, I made my way down the concrete path as she climbed into the driver's seat behind the wheel of our green Pontiac.

Mother pressed the gas pedal, and we gained speed. I always watched closely because I wanted **my license** by my sixteenth birthday—only three months away. I knew the process well by now. She had guided me through practice sessions in the parking lot next to the grocery store often enough.

We moved through the streets in silence, listening to the newsman's descriptions of the crowds gathering at Central High. I noticed some of our neighbors standing on the sidewalk, many more than were usually out this time of day.

"That's strange," Mama mumbled as she waved to people

....

voiced talked about
lingered waited
blinked back tears tried not to cry
my license to get my driver's license

who didn't bother waving back. "No matter, maybe they didn't see me." Our neighbors had always been so friendly, but now they peered at us without their usual smiles. Then I saw Kathy and Ronda, two of my school friends, standing with their mothers. Anxious to catch their attention, I waved out the window with a loud "Hi." Their disapproving glances matched those of the adults.

"I didn't do anything to them," I said, not understanding their reason.

"Then you don't have anything to be concerned about." Mother Lois **maneuvered** through the unusually heavy traffic. "I don't know where all the cars could have come from," she said. We both **craned our necks**, curious about all the unfamiliar cars and people. Certainly there had never before been so many white people driving down the streets of our quiet, tree-lined neighborhood.

The voice on the radio grew more **urgent** as the announcer described the ranks of Arkansas National Guardsmen who **ringed** Central High School. Hearing the news as we drew near our destination, Mother said, "I think I'll park here. The meeting place is quite a ways away, but from the looks of things we won't get any closer."

The announcer said it was 7:55 as Mama squeezed into a parking space, and we settled ourselves quietly for a moment, trying to identify the buzzing noise that seemed as if it were all around us. It resembled the sound of crowds at my high school football games. But how could that be? The announcer said

....

maneuvered moved
craned our necks looked around us
urgent serious and worried
ringed surrounded

there was a crowd, but surely it couldn't be that big.

Anxious to see the familiar faces of our friends or some of our own people, we hurried up the block lined with wood-frame houses and screened-in porches. I strained to see what lay ahead of us. In the distance, large crowds of white people were **lining the curb** directly across from the front of Central High. As we approached behind them, we could see only the clusters of white people that stretched for a distance of two blocks along the entire span of the school building. My mind could take in the sights and sounds only one by one: flashing cameras, voices shouting in my ears, men and women **jostling** each other, old people, young people, people running, uniformed police officers walking, men standing still, men and women waving their fists, and then the long line of uniformed soldiers carrying weapons just like in the war movies I had seen.

Everyone's attention seemed **riveted** on the center of the line of soldiers where a big commotion was taking place. At first we couldn't see what they were looking at. People were shouting and pointing, and the noise hurt my ears and muffled the words. We couldn't understand what they were saying. As we drew near, the angry outbursts became even more intense, and we began to hear their words more clearly. "Niggers, go home! Niggers, go back where you belong!"

I stood motionless, stunned by the hurtful words. I searched for something to **hang on to**, something familiar that would comfort me or make sense, but there was nothing.

"Two, four, six, eight, we ain't gonna integrate!" Over and

....

lining the curb standing on the side of the street
jostling pushing, shoving
riveted focused
hang on to understand

over, the words rang out. The terrifying frenzy of the crowd was building like steam in an erupting volcano.

"We have to find the others," Mama yelled in my ear. "We'll be safer with the group." She grabbed my arm to pull me forward, out of my **trance**. The look on her face mirrored the terror I felt. Some of the white men and women standing around us seemed to be observing anxiously. Others with angry faces and wide-open mouths were screaming their rage. Their words were becoming increasingly **vile, fueled by** whatever was happening directly in front of the school.

The sun beat down on our heads as we made our way through the crowd, searching for our friends. Most people ignored us, jostling each other and craning their necks to see whatever was at the center of the furor. Finally, we got closer to the **hub** of activity. Standing on our toes, we stretched as tall as we could to see what everyone was watching.

"Oh, my Lord," Mother said.

It was my friend Elizabeth they were watching. The anger of that huge crowd was directed toward Elizabeth Eckford as she stood alone, in front of Central High, facing the long line of soldiers, with a huge crowd of white people screeching at her back. Barely five feet tall, Elizabeth cradled her books in her arms as she desperately searched for the right place to enter. Soldiers in uniforms and helmets, cradling their rifles, towered over her. Slowly she walked first to one and then another opening in their line. Each time she approached, the soldiers **closed ranks**, shutting her out. As she turned toward us, her

....

trance shock
vile, fueled by evil because of
hub center
closed ranks moved together

eyes hidden by dark glasses, we could see how erect and proud she stood despite the fear she must have been feeling.

As Elizabeth walked along the line of guardsmen, they did nothing to protect her from **her stalkers**. When a crowd of fifty or more closed in like diving vultures, the soldiers stared straight ahead, as if posing for a photograph. Once more Elizabeth stood still, stunned, not knowing what to do. The people surrounding us shouted, stomped, and whistled as though her **awful predicament were a** triumph for them.

I wanted to help her, but the human wall in front of us would not be moved. We could only wedge through partway. Finally, we realized our efforts were futile; we could only pray as we watched her struggle to survive. People began to applaud and shout, "Get her, get the nigger out of there. Hang her black ass!" Not one of those white adults attempted to rescue Elizabeth. The hulking soldiers continued to observe her peril like spectators enjoying a spoil.

Under **siege**, Elizabeth slowly made her way toward the bench at the bus stop. Looking straight ahead as she walked, she did not acknowledge the people yelping at her heels, like mad dogs. Mother and I looked at each other, suddenly conscious that we, too, were trapped by a violent **mob**.

Ever so slowly, we eased our way backward through the crowd, being careful not to attract attention. But a white man clawed at me, grabbing my sleeve and yelling, "We got us a nigger right here!" Just then another man tugged at his arm distracting him. Somehow I managed to scramble away. As a

....

her stalkers her attackers; the screaming white people
awful predicament were a being trapped was a
siege attack
mob crowd of angry people

commotion began building around us, Mother took my arm, and we moved fast, sometimes crouching to avoid attracting more attention.

We gained some distance from the center of the crowd and made our way down the block. But when I looked back, I saw a man following us, yelling, "They're getting away! Those niggers are getting away!" Pointing to us, he **enlisted** others to join him. Now we were being chased by four men, and their number was growing.

We scurried down the sidewalk, bumping into people. Most of the crowd was still preoccupied watching Elizabeth. Panic-stricken, I wanted to shout for help. But I knew it would do no good. Policemen stood by watching Elizabeth being **accosted**. Why would they help us?

"Melba, take these keys," Mother commanded as she tossed them at me. "Get to the car. Leave without me if you have to."

I plucked the car keys from the air. "No, Mama, I won't go without you." Suddenly I felt the sting of her hand as it struck the side of my face. She had never slapped me before. "Do what I say!" she shouted. Still, I knew I couldn't leave her there. I reached back to take her arm. Her pace was slowing, and I tried to pull her forward. The men were **gaining on** us. If we yelled for help or made any fuss, others might join our attackers. Running faster, I felt myself begin to **wear out**. I didn't have enough breath to keep moving so fast. My knees hurt, my calves were aching, but the car was just around the next corner.

The men chasing us were joined by another carrying a rope.

....

enlisted got, found
accosted attacked
gaining on getting closer to
wear out get tired

At times, **our pursuers** were so close I could look back and see the anger in their eyes. Mama's pace slowed, and one man came close enough to touch her. He grabbed for her arm but instead tugged at her blouse. The fabric ripped, and he fell backward. Mama stepped out of her high-heeled shoes, leaving them behind, her pace quickening in stocking feet.

One of the men closest to me swung at me with a large tree branch but missed. I felt even more panic rise up in my throat. If he hit me hard enough to knock me over, **I would be at his mercy**. I could hear Grandma India's voice saying, God is always with you, even when things seem awful. I felt a surge of strength and **a new wind**. As I turned the corner, our car came into sight. I ran hard—faster than ever before—unlocked the door, and jumped in.

Mother was struggling, barely able to keep ahead of her attackers. I could see them turning the corner close on her heels, moving fast toward us. I swung open the passenger door for Mother and **revved** the engine. Barely waiting for her to shut the door, I shoved the gearshift into reverse and backed down the street with more speed than I'd ever driven forward. I slowed to back around the corner. One of the men caught up and pounded his fists on the hood of our car, while another threw a brick at the windshield.

Turning left, we gained speed as we drove through a hail of shouts and stones and glaring faces. But I knew I would make it because the car was moving fast and Mama was with me.

We sped away from Central High School's neighborhood

....

our pursuers the people chasing us
I would be at his mercy he could do anything to me
a new wind had more energy
revved started

and into more familiar streets where we should have felt safe. Mother directed me not to drive straight home but to circle around until we knew for certain that the men from the mob weren't chasing us. Even though I didn't have a license and had only practiced driving in the parking lot, she wouldn't allow me to stop so we could switch places. Her face **was drained** and her eyes haunted by a kind of fear I had not seen in her before.

As I drove, I couldn't help noticing that the streets were **clogged** with cars and people that did not belong in our neighborhood. There were dust-covered trucks full of tobacco-chewing white men, their naked arms and shoulders sporting tattoos. When we pulled into our backyard, Grandmother India was waiting for us with an anxious expression. "Thank God, you made it home," she gasped.

"What about Elizabeth and the others? Have you heard anything?"

"Yes, yes, but let's get inside. Hurry, child. Hurry." Grandma India **ushered** us through the back door. As we entered the house, I saw that she had locked all the doors and windows and pulled all of the shades. As soon as we were safely inside, she piled chairs against the locked back door.

"So what about Elizabeth?" I said.

"I think she's safe. A white woman and man sat with her on the bus bench, protecting her from those awful people clawing at her. Then they got on the bus with her and rode away, so she's okay."

"And the others—Terry and Ernie and those guys?"

------

was drained looked exhausted
clogged filled
ushered led

"The soldiers turned them away from that school just like they did Elizabeth. They're safe. They didn't catch as much trouble, because they were in a large group with Mrs. Bates and some of those ministers. But still they didn't have **no Sunday picnic**; they had to get out of there real fast."

Even though Mother looked exhausted, **nothing would do for her but** to get dressed and go to work. "We've got to lead as normal a life as possible," she argued as we described to Grandma what had happened to us.

"One report said those troops were armed with rifles, nightsticks, and bayonets. Did you see any of that, Melba?"

"Uh, yes, ma'am. I think I saw guns."

"Maybe things got mixed up. Perhaps the governor had them there to keep peace, and they mixed up their orders," Grandma mused.

"Seems to me they had ample opportunity to keep peace by protecting Elizabeth." Mother Lois sounded very angry. "I think this situation is different than what we **bargained for**. We'd better let things **cool off a bit**. You can go back to Horace Mann for now."

Grandma squared her shoulders and said, "I don't see how that will solve anything. Pretty soon, white folks will think it's as okay to enslave us as it is to use soldiers to keep our kids out of school."

Mother stood in silence, pondering Grandma's words for a long moment. Her expression reflected the painful realization that maybe what Grandma said was true. And then suddenly

....

no Sunday picnic an easy time
nothing would do for her but she decided
bargained for expected
cool off a bit settle down; become less dangerous

she said, "I had almost forgotten; I have to speak to you, Melba, and I want you to listen closely to every word and obey. Under no circumstances must you ever mention to anyone what happened to us this morning. Even if you have to tell a **white lie** and say we didn't go to Central, we have to keep this our secret."

Telling a white lie was something she'd never before given me permission to do. She swore me to absolute silence, saying above all else those men must not **connect us with their ugly deed**. If we told the story and they found out who they were chasing, they might come after us to **finish the job**. As she spoke, her voice quavered and her hands shook. I had never seen her so uncontrolled. She looked the way I felt, battered and weary. Finally, she instructed, "Melba, don't you dare go outside, girl. I want to know where you are every moment." She pulled on her jacket, peeked through the glass in the front door, then hurried out onto the porch, almost running around the house to the car.

I resigned myself to the fact that Grandma wouldn't allow me to visit Thelma or Minnijean or any other friends who lived nearby. I wanted to call them for more news of what happened to them, but before I could pick up the receiver, the phone began to ring off the hook.

"Don't you dare answer," Grandma shouted to me from the kitchen.

"I think I want to go back to Horace Mann," I told my grandmother. "At least I'll have assignments and friends and all

....

white lie small lie

connect us with their ugly deed know that we were the people they were chasing and threatening

finish the job really hurt us

sorts of wonderful first school day things to do."

"One little **setback**—and you want out," she said. **"Naw, you're not a quitter."**

In my diary I wrote:

*I was disappointed not to see what is inside Central High School.
I don't understand why the governor sent grown-up soldiers to keep us out.
I don't know if I should go back.
But Grandma is right, if I don't go back, they will think they have won. They will think they can use soldiers to frighten us, and we'll always have to obey them. They'll always be in charge if I don't go back to Central and make the integration happen.*

By late afternoon the ringing phone, the hot weather, and **my confinement were driving me nuts**, so when the phone rang, I grabbed for it.

"Where were you?" I could hear annoyance in Minnijean's voice.

"I was there," I said. "Across the street. I saw Elizabeth being chased by those ugly people. Why was she alone?"

"Remember, she doesn't have a phone, so she didn't get that midnight call. She didn't know where or when to meet us."

"Mama and I barely made it out of there!" I said, being cautious not to tell all.

"We got outta there as fast as we could. First we went to the superintendent's office. We waited there for an hour, sitting

....

setback problem, delay

"Naw, you're not a quitter." "No, you are not a person who quits. You will not give up."

my confinement were driving me nuts being made to stay in the house were really bothering me on those hard benches. Then Mrs. Bates **dragged us on** to the United States Attorney's office, to see a Mr. Cobb."

"Why?"

"She said since Judge Davies made a federal order, we should go there, but Cobb sent us on to the **FBI** office. That was kind of secret and fun. Those guys look just the way they do on television, like they know something but they won't tell."

"Yeah, but what did they do?"

"Asked a lot of questions and wrote the answers down."

"Questions?"

"Yeah, all about where we stood and who did what to us. Took hours and I was sweating so bad I thought I would die."

"Well, are they gonna do anything?"

"**Investigate**, they said they'd investigate."

"Sure, by that time we could be dead."

"**You ain't kidding.** That mob was outright nasty. I gotta go now, but can you meet me in fifteen minutes and we'll go to the community center?"

"The community center," I whispered. It seemed like forever since I'd had an ordinary afternoon there, listening to records and talking to friends who didn't use the word "integration." I thought about the wonderful times Minnijean and I had shared—times when our greatest concern was saving enough allowance to buy a new record or praying to be asked to walk to the cafeteria with the right boy. Maybe our lives could be that way again. I tiptoed past Grandma, peacefully snoozing in her rocking chair. Suddenly she was awake. "Just where do you

....

dragged us on took us

FBI special police agency; Federal Bureau of Investigation

Investigate Find out what happened

You ain't kidding. You are right.

think you're going, Missy?"

"Uh, to the community center. I didn't want to disturb you. I thought you were sleeping."

"Uh, huh. Have a seat. The best you can do is let up a window. But you ain't going to no community center."

I couldn't stop the rush of tears. I ran to my room and fell onto the bed, burying my face in the pillow to hide the sobs that **wrenched my insides**. All my disappointment over not getting into Central High and the mob chase as well as the big sudden changes in my life over the past few weeks **came crashing in on me**.

Then I heard Grandma India padding across the room and felt the weight of her body shift the plane of the mattress as she sat down.

"You had a good cry, girl?" Her voice was sympathetic but also one sliver away from being angry.

"Yes, ma'am."

"You'll make this your last cry. You're **a warrior on the battlefield for your Lord**. God's warriors don't cry, 'cause they *t, t₂* trust that he's always by their side. The women of this family don't break down in the face of trouble. We act with courage, and with God's help, we ship trouble right on out."

"But I—" I tried to explain.

"But nothing. Now, you **get yourself together**, read the Twenty-Third Psalm, and don't ever let me see you behave this way again."

"Yes, ma'am." The anger in her voice hurt my feelings, but

---

wrenched my insides shook my whole body

came crashing in on me suddenly became very real

a warrior on the battlefield for your Lord fighting for an important cause

get yourself together calm down

her warm hand patted my arm to reassure me of her love. From then on, I knew I could only cry when no one would hear me.

The shrill ring of the telephone upset me even more now that I had seen my enemies. I imagined the callers to resemble those men who had chased me. It felt as though they were entering my home each time they called. I could tell Mother felt the same way. With each ring, her expression turned **grimmer**.

"I'll get it." Conrad's voice was less enthusiastic than usual, but still he made his chase for the phone until he was ordered to halt. Grandma had interrupted her cooking to hurry to the phone.

She called to me from the hallway. "Sounds like maybe that boy Vince. You know, the polite one from church that we usually see at the wrestling matches." Grandma beckoned me to take the receiver.

Vince, I thought to myself **as my heart leaped with joy**. Sure, I knew very well who Vince was. He attended high school in a neighboring town, but he was in my Sunday school class. It was Grandma who didn't really know that Vince was my secret, pretend **dreamboat** boyfriend. I wasn't at all certain he knew it. He was at least two years older than me and drove a new Chevy and looked sort of like a caramel-colored James Darren.

"Make this conversation brief, honey," Grandma said as she handed me the phone.

....

grimmer more upset; more worried

as my heart leaped with joy and felt very happy

dreamboat handsome

"Hello," I said, using the sexy whisper **dictated** by romance magazines.

"Melba?" It wasn't Vince's voice saying my name.

"Yes," I answered in a polite tone, **dropping my pretense**. The voice wasn't at all familiar to me.

"Melba, nigger, I know where you live . . . Twelfth and Cross. We gonna get you tonight . . . 'long about midnight." I heard the receiver click, and he was gone. Did he know where my bedroom was? Would he come over now? Did he have a bomb? I couldn't tell Mama and the others that he knew so much about us, so I choked back my tears.

As I entered the living room, faces turned my way **in anticipation**. I pretended a smile and said it was somebody else, another friend, not Vince.

I thought it was a sign that we were feeling more confident when we turned the television set off in the middle of the uproar about Central and took our places at the dinner table. After the blessing, the topic turned to what was really on our minds.

"I'll keep watch again tonight," Grandma said.

Mother studied her plate for a long moment before she looked up at Grandma. "Maybe you could get some sleep tonight, and I could stand guard?"

"That would be a real good idea except you don't know how to shoot a gun. This is no time **for on-the-job training**."

....

dictated recommended
dropping my pretense no longer pretending to be sexy
in anticipation to hear what Vince said
for on-the-job training to teach you

Grandma was **an expert marksman**. As a railroad man, Grandpa had spent lots of time away from home. He had insisted Grandma learn to use a gun to protect herself because they had lived in an **isolated area** in the early years of their marriage. "God does not forgive those who kill others," Grandma said. "Expert marksmanship is a must because you always got to aim for fingers or toes, and them's small targets."

....

an expert marksman excellent at shooting guns

isolated area area that was far away from other people

BEFORE YOU MOVE ON...

1. **Summarize** How did Melba and her mother get away from the angry mob?

2. **Paraphrase** Reread page 63. What did Grandma India mean when she said, "God's warriors don't cry"?

LOOK AHEAD Read pages 67–81 to find out how Melba feels about her decision to attend Central.

5

Dear Diary,

*The two days since I first went to Central felt like I was living in some stranger's life. Today I won't think of integration, I won't think of Central High, and I won't think of the white people. I will spend the whole day finding the perfect **disguise to wear to** the wrestling matches. . . .*

No matter what, I'm gonna be a regular person. I'm gonna have my usual date with Grandma and my secret, pretend date with Vince at the matches.

As hard as I tried not to care, I couldn't start my morning without knowing what the governor, his National Guard, and the school board were **up to**. I had to face the awful truth. Grandma was right, I was letting those people **determine** how I felt, and how I lived a great part of my day. I brushed my hair back into a ponytail and headed for the front porch. As I picked up the newspaper, headlines **leaped out at me.**

....

disguise to wear to clothes to make me look different at
up to doing and saying
determine tell me; decide
leaped out at me caught my attention

HALT IN INTEGRATION ASKED: BOARD SEEKS SUSPENSION OF U.S. ORDER

The Little Rock School Board was asking Judge Davies to **suspend temporarily** the plan for integrating Central High. He would be holding a hearing on their petition on Friday, September 6, today.

As I read on, I saw the good news.

IKE SAYS HE WILL USE LAW. TELLS FAUBUS: COOPERATE WITH US

"The federal Constitution will be **upheld by every legal means at my command**," President Eisenhower had told Governor Faubus. The President had sent a telegram to Governor Faubus saying he was sure the governor, the National Guard, and other state officials would give full cooperation to the United States Supreme Court. The President also reassured the governor that rumors of federal authorities waiting to arrest him were untrue.

"I think the school board's **backing off** having the integration," I told my mother as she prepared to leave for school.

"Be patient," Mother said, heading toward the car. "By the way, I'm counting on you to give your grandmother extra special help today. She's a bit weary."

Oh, no, I especially didn't want Grandmother India to be

....

suspend temporarily delay

upheld by every legal means at my command followed, and I will use every power I have to make you follow it

backing off deciding against

weary. I **was counting on** her to take me to the wrestling matches. For the rest of the day, I **devoted myself to** doing more than my share of the chores. I would do anything to keep her able-bodied and fit.

As Saturday morning turned into afternoon, I was busy keeping to myself so I could apply my grown-up makeup. It was an art I had not yet acquired since I wasn't allowed to wear makeup. Even by the third try I resembled a circus clown. But as I looked in the mirror for a final check, I was proud of the job I had done. I was a new person. R P

Promptly at five, Grandma breezed into the front hall. She was dressed in churchgoing clothes, her Ladies Day outfit, a blue suit with a matching hat that swooped down from its mischievous perch on the side of her head.

"Well, don't just stand there, child, help me find my parasol." I couldn't help smiling. The frantic search for the umbrella was a familiar scene. It made me feel that at least some part of my life was **left intact**.

"We'd better go without it," I said. We were running late, and if we didn't hurry, the bus would leave us behind. I had been patiently waiting, hoping that at any moment my grandmother would **signal her approval of** my grown-up outfit, upswept hairdo, and high-heeled black patent shoes. Layers of forbidden makeup and dark glasses completed what I thought was the perfect disguise. The white people would never, ever recognize me from any picture they might have seen. Of course, my one big worry was that Grandma might say it was too grown-up, but R P

....

was counting on wanted
devoted myself to spent my time
left intact still the same
signal her approval of say she liked

she only peered at me with a strange and lingering expression.

"Let's go, Grandma, we're gonna be late," I said, trying to **coax** her toward the front door. I was praying Vince wouldn't grow impatient waiting for me and leave, or, worse yet, allow himself to be talked into spending the evening with one of the other girls.

"Why don't you **take a seat**. I'll be back in a moment," Grandma said, sounding quite strange, beckoning me to remain there in the hallway by the door. I heard her and Mama whispering in the other room. As I settled into a chair, I thought about all the earlier times when we had gone together to the wrestling matches.

Those matches were big events in my life because we traveled downtown to the Robinson Auditorium, a place usually reserved for white people only. Those were the times when I got to go outside my neighborhood, outside the world where I spent most of my life. We sat in the same room with white folks, able to observe them close up. I wanted to get to know them better, to see **what it was they had that put them in charge**.

Grandma India would adjust her hat, and then we would both strut down the aisle to the seats that her friend Mr. Claxton had saved for us. He would always be there waiting for us with the best balcony seats our people were allowed to have.

After we got settled, I would complain about my thirst, and Grandma would grant permission for a trip to the soft-drink stand. There I would meet Vince, as we'd planned, and take him to join Grandma and Mr. Claxton, explaining that our

....

coax move

take a seat sit down

what it was they had that put them in charge why they got to make all of the rules meeting had been accidental. I had enjoyed eight evenings of double-dating with Grandma and Vince, and she didn't even realize it. I knew **full well** my family would never have allowed me to date. They had said all along that when I was eighteen and going to college, I could go out with boys, and then only in the company of **a chaperon**.

As the evening **wore on** and the matches got really heated, Grandma India and I would behave as we behaved nowhere else. She would pound the floor with her parasol and shout and wave her fist until her hat was twisted on her head and her churchgoing outfit was rumpled. Once she had even dropped her glasses and broken them in a fit of rage when her tag-team favorites, Mud Mountain and Blue Moon Hog, were counted out by the referee.

When it was all over, she would **revert** to her quietest and most cultured tone, speaking barely above a whisper. "Magnificent, child. That's the way a body gets rid of aggression without misbehaving. Now, Melba, straighten yourself up, honey, time to present ourselves as the ladies we are."

"Sorry, child, you can't go with me to the matches, not tonight," said Grandma, grabbing me from my happy recollections. "Maybe next time, when the integration settles down."

"But why not?" I felt tears coming, but I had promised Grandma I wouldn't cry.

....

full well without a doubt; very well that
a chaperon an adult
wore on continued
revert go back; return

"It's just too dangerous for you to go there amongst all those white people."

"They'll never recognize me—see, see!" I twirled about to show her that I was really a new person.

Grandma India moved closer to me and cupped my face in her hands, "You're staying home, baby. It's for your own good."

"Everything's being taken from me!" I cried.

"Your grandmother's right, honey." Mother Lois put her arm around my waist, trying to convince me it was not **the end of the world**. "Suppose one of those people who saw us at Central recognizes you and tries to **pick** a fight? What about the risk to your grandmother?"

"I'll never go back to Central!" I ran from the room and locked my bedroom door, burying my face in the pillow so no one could hear me cry. Later, I wrote in my diary:

Freedom is not integration. . . .
Freedom is being able to go with Grandma to the wrestling matches.

The next day, in the Sunday paper. I saw a pitiful close-up photograph of Elizabeth, walking alone in front of Central on that first day of integration. It **pained my insides** to see, once again, the twisted, scowling white faces with open mouths jeering, clustered about my friend's head like bouquets of grotesque flowers. It was an ad paid for by a white man from a small town in Arkansas. "If you live in Arkansas," the ad read,

....

the end of the world that terrible
pick start
pained my insides hurt me

"study this picture and know shame. When hate is unleashed and **bigotry finds a voice**, God help us all."

I felt a kind of joy and hope in the thought that one white man was willing to use his own money to call attention to the injustice we were facing. Maybe the picture would help others realize that what they were doing was hurting everybody.

Seeing that ad was the beginning of a wonderful Sunday. Just before church started, Vince walked right up and said to me flat-out, "I want you to be my girlfriend." ⟵

"Girlfriend?" I repeated the word, desperately groping to find just the right response. I'd never been asked before.

As the sermon began, I felt guilty that I didn't have my mind on prayer. Instead, I was wondering whether Vince would give me a friendship ring or **the letter from his sweater**. It pushed all thoughts of Central High, Governor Faubus, and integration into the back of my mind.

The minister was urging us to pray for Governor Faubus and do whatever was necessary to heal any sour feelings we had against white people. He had been organizing other ministers in Little Rock to speak out and condemn the governor for dispatching the troops. He said we should pray for the judges and city officials and the President to make the right decisions—to let us into Central High.

Suddenly my attention was drawn to what the prayer ladies were saying. They were calling my name, asking God to protect me when I walked into **the lion's den** at Central. I remembered what Grandma had said: "Church is the **life's blood** of our

....

bigotry finds a voice prejudiced people are listened to
the letter from his sweater ask me to date him
the lion's den danger
life's blood center, foundation

73

folks' community."

I knew very well that without the church and the help of the people sitting around me, I had little chance of making it through that school year. Certainly I couldn't count on the police. If I got into trouble and really needed protection, it would probably be the network of phone calls initiated by Reverend Young that would set off a rescue and **construct a web of safety**.

U.S. COURT SUMMONS SERVED ON GOVERNOR
—*Arkansas Gazette*, Wednesday, September 11, 1957

A week after our first attempt to get into Central, I was still rushing to get each morning's newspaper to read about the people who gathered daily in front of the school to see that we didn't get in. The President had agreed to give the governor **a ten-day respite to sort out** his response to the court order. There would be a meeting at Eisenhower's vacation spot in Rhode Island after that.

The next day we learned that Representative Brooks Hays would go with Governor Faubus to a five-man conference that included the President, Attorney General Herbert Brownell, Jr., and Sherman Adams, Chief White House Assistant.

On September 15, the *Arkansas Gazette* headlines read:

....

construct a web of safety keep me safe
a ten-day respite to sort out ten days to decide on

FAUBUS ASKING COMPROMISE, IKE REFUSES COMMITMENT; STATUS OF TROOPS STILL UNANSWERED

Realizing that the dilemma of integration wasn't going to be resolved quickly, everybody seemed to be concerned about our falling behind in our schoolwork. Teachers from our community along with other professionals were offering to give us books and to tutor us. Grace Lorch, who had helped Elizabeth escape the mob, and her husband, Dr. Lorch, organized tutoring sessions. It felt good to dress in school clothes and go to Philander Smith, our community's college. For part of each day, I studied schoolwork and spent time with my eight friends, enjoying a **thimbleful of normality**. RP

Being together in those classes, the nine of us were developing a true friendship—becoming **closer knit** than we might have been under other circumstances. We talked about our fears, what we missed at our old school, and our hopes that the integration issues would soon be resolved. While I regretted the friendships I was losing, I **cherished the growing ties** to the eight.

Just before the court hearing where Governor Faubus would be **called to account**, the nine of us were summoned to Mrs. Bates's house to meet with the press. Nothing had changed since our last meeting. The troops were still in place around the school, and every morning the crowd of segregationists grew larger. Governor Faubus was still predicting violence.

....

thimbleful of normality little bit of normal life
closer knit better friends
cherished the growing ties valued my friendship
called to account forced to explain his actions

Several very dignified and important-looking men sat in her living room. One was the NAACP attorney, Wiley Branton. I recognized another man whose picture I'd seen in the newspapers: the famous lawyer Thurgood Marshall, the man who had delivered the argument that resulted in the Supreme Court's 1954 school integration ruling.

Judging by my father's height, I figured Mr. Marshall was more than six feet tall, with a **commanding** presence, fair skin, and brown hair and mustache. He spoke like somebody on television, his sharp, quick New York accent overlaying a slight Southern drawl. "At the same time we are petitioning for a court order to force your governor to move his troops away from Central's front door, we'll be planning other options. Meanwhile we are asking that you be patient. Justice will **prevail**." He spoke confidently, in a way that made me feel that I deserved to be admitted to Central High.

I looked at this man who seemed to have none of the fears and hesitation of my parents or the other adults around us. Instead he had a **self-assured air about him** as though he had seen the promised land and knew for certain we could get there. We had only heard rumors of freedom, but he had lived it, and it showed in his every word, his every movement, in the way he sat tall in his seat.

He urged us to prepare ourselves to **testify** in federal court, if need be. Right then and there I began to fret about the truth I couldn't tell. If I testified in court about what really happened to me, it would get printed in the newspapers, and those men

....

commanding powerful

prevail win, succeed

self-assured air about him confident attitude

testify tell our side of the story; give evidence

would come after us again. But now I knew that, worst of all, it would give the governor yet another excuse to keep us out of school. The very basis of his argument against our integrating was that it would cause so much violence that blood would run in the streets. If I told the judge about the men having chased us, the governor could use my words as weapons against us.

But as I listened to Mr. Marshall speak, I felt much better. His positive attitude gave me hope that even if I couldn't speak my truth, the **scales of justice were weighted on our side**. I had read that he had faced up to other Southern segregationists and forced them to let **my people run for public office**. He had also fought for equal rights for women. I felt honored that he would take the time and energy to fight for our rights. There was no doubt in my mind that if any soul on this earth could get us into Central High, this great man, Mr. Thurgood Marshall, was the one.

During the meeting, the upstairs had filled with a throng of news people, most of them white, with just a **sprinkling of our people**. We students were directed to take our seats and to answer questions as clearly and briefly as possible. For the first time, we were introduced as the Little Rock Nine.

Cameras flashed, bright lights stung my eyes, and reporters asked lots of questions for the next half hour. Many of the reporters asked the attorneys what they planned to do to get rid of the troops. And questions were directed to Elizabeth. She seemed shy about answering, but with Mrs. Bates's help, she forced herself to say a few words. Eventually, however,

....

scales of justice were weighted on our side law supported our right to go to Central High

my people run for public office African Americans work for the government

sprinkling of our people few African Americans

questions were directed to all of us. My heart raced with fear and anticipation as I observed the process. **I was almost hypnotized by the wonder of it all.**

"Miss Pattillo, how do you feel about going back to Central High?"

"Miss," I whispered as my hands perspired and my knees shook. Thoughts buzzed inside my head like bees disturbed in their hive. It was the first time anybody white had ever called me Miss. They cared what I thought. I struggled to find a **suitable** answer.

"We have a right to go to that school, and I'm certain our governor, who was elected to govern all the people, will decide to do what is **just**." I felt myself speak aloud before I was ready. Who said that? It sounded like me, but the words . . . where had they come from? The white reporters wrote my words down and behaved as if what I said was very important. Pride welled up inside me, and for the first time, I knew that working for integration was the right thing for me to be doing.

"Mrs. Pattillo, how does a mother decide to send her daughter into such a dangerous situation?" Mother Lois was sitting, shy and quiet, in a shadowed corner of the room. I could tell she was startled by the question; nevertheless she stood and said, "Indeed it is a hard decision—but we are a Christian family, with absolute faith that God will protect her, no matter what."

After the main session, reporters pulled each one of us students aside for what they called **one-on-one** interviews.

....

I was almost hypnotized by the wonder of it all. It was amazing to me.

suitable good

just fair, right

one-on-one individual, private

Listening to all the talk about our being heroes and heroines made me proud of Mama and Grandma and all of us. I wished Grandma could tell the reporters how she stood guard. Then they would know she was a heroine, too.

When the conference **broke up**, I lingered in a quiet corner, **soaking up** the sights and sounds around me. I was fascinated by the way the reporters wrote so fast in their narrow notebooks and spoke into their hand-held tape recorders. The way they responded to me made me feel equal to the white reporters. They looked me directly in the eye. I never saw any sign they were thinking of calling me a nigger. Some of them looked at me with admiring eyes and answered all my questions about their work without making me feel silly for asking. They also behaved as though they were genuine friends with the people of color among their ranks, sharing work and laughter.

I felt a new **fountain** of hope rise up inside me. Just maybe, I thought to myself, just maybe this is what I want to be when I grow up. If I were a news reporter, I could be in charge of a few things.

That night I wrote in my diary:

Today is the first time in my life I felt equal to white people. I want more of that feeling. I'll do whatever I have to do to keep feeling equal all the time.

I apologize, God, for thinking you had taken away all my normal life. Maybe you're just exchanging it for a new life.

....

broke up ended
soaking up paying attention to
fountain sense, feeling

HOPE OF SETTLEMENT FADES AS GOVERNOR FACES DAY IN COURT

—*Arkansas Gazette*, Thursday, September 19, 1957

The town was crowded with journalists from around the world. The federal court hearing would be one of the most significant in history—a **precedent-setting** decision could be made that affected the whole country. That's what all the newspaper reporters and radio announcers said over and over again. States'-rights advocates from surrounding Southern towns were **up in arms**. They were headed for Little Rock to add to the **incendiary** feelings in our town.

The segregationists were doing a lot of newspaper advertising to get people to participate in their rallies. The Arkansas National Guard remained at Central High, and **hooligans rampaged** through the streets. In particular they preyed on our people walking alone in isolated areas or at night. A new level of tension crept into our own household, nearly overwhelming me. I found it difficult to study, difficult to concentrate. Some days it was as though someone had put me in Grandma's cake mixer, but I was struggling to be still, not to spin or shudder or shake.

During those rare moments when I sat alone in my room among my stuffed animals, I daydreamed about Vince and what it would be like to be his ordinary girlfriend and have real dates. I had finally gathered the nerve to ask Mother and Grandma for permission to date. After giving me what amounted to

....

precedent-setting very important

up in arms very angry

incendiary angry, violent

hooligans rampaged people trying to cause trouble ran

a thorough exam with really hard questions about Vince's intentions and character, Mother Lois said, "Have him come to the house." Her expression saddened as she went on: "Now understand, this is not really dating, and you can only see this boy in the presence of another adult. I'm allowing you to do this because integration has taken away so much of **your social life**."

I had a hard time containing my **hallelujah** shouts as I started to leave the room. But just as I reached the door, she said, "Of course, you'll wait to **exercise this privilege** until after the court hearing tomorrow."

On the night before the hearing, I took Grandma's advice and let God worry about what was going to happen in that courtroom.

I wrote in my diary:

> *Dear God, We can't get along without you. Governor Faubus has lots of attorneys and the paper says they have more than two hundred witnesses. I'm counting on you once and for all to make it clear whether you want me in that school.* ***Thy will be done.***

....

your social life the things you do for fun
hallelujah happy, joyous
exercise this privilege do this
Thy will be done. *Whatever*
God wants is what will happen.

BEFORE YOU MOVE ON...

1. **Inference** Why did Melba feel that everything was being taken from her?

2. **Mood** Reread pages 78–79. How did the mood of the story change when the reporters questioned Melba?

LOOK AHEAD Which side won the court case? Read pages 82–90 to find out.

6

FAUBUS, U.S. GOVERNMENT HEAD INTO CRUCIAL
COLLISION IN FEDERAL COURT TODAY
—Arkansas Gazette, Friday, September 20, 1957

Sitting alone in my room, I couldn't stop thinking how
Governor Faubus would **for certain** have to be in that
courtroom. I couldn't imagine that he wouldn't be there. In my
diary I wrote:

> *This is the day I hope to meet Governor Faubus **face to face**.
> I can't decide what to say to him. If only he will listen to me one
> minute, I know I can make him understand there is nothing
> so bad about me that he shouldn't allow white children to go to
> school with me.*

The nine of us walked up the sidewalk toward the Federal
Building **at a brisk pace**. Our group included Mrs. Bates,
attorneys Thurgood Marshall and Wiley Branton, and a number
of people I did not know. I was told they were community

....

COLLISION CONFLICT
for certain definitely
face to face in person
at a brisk pace very quickly

ministers and lawyers, coming along to protect us. Between **awkward scraps** of conversation, I could hear our footsteps on the sidewalk as we moved toward the official-looking building. I had never paid much attention to it before.

I was **a bit on edge**. A small part of me was becoming accustomed to the fact that since the integration had begun, both my people and whites stared at me. Some of the faces lining the streets on that morning had welcome smiles, others were indifferent, while still others were undeniably angry. I wore dark glasses, which allowed me to peer out wherever I wanted without anybody being able to see how fearful I was.

"We're going to have to take the kids in through the side door," a man's voice said. My pace quickened as we were ushered past all the people milling about, through a very narrow, dimly lit marble hall, where our voices and footsteps echoed. We were led to the elevator, walking fast as if we were being chased. The door slid shut, and I stared straight ahead. My knees were trembling, and every inch of my body was perspiring. That elevator was so full that I could hear its **guts grinding** as it struggled to deliver us to the fourth-floor courtroom.

I hoped the opening elevator doors would admit fresh air. Instead, they revealed a crush of people, jammed body to body. I was blinded by the glaring lights held high over the heads of the sea of people by news photographers trying to get pictures. We could hardly get out of the elevator and into the **throng**. Like sardines we wiggled and pushed, trying to forge a pathway. I stopped thinking about fresh, cool air; I just wanted to breathe

....

awkward scraps uncomfortable moments
a bit on edge nervous, anxious
guts grinding mechanical parts moving
throng crowd of people

and not be crushed. As we emerged, several reporters started shouting questions at us. I felt as though I were attending one of those Hollywood openings I'd seen on TV.

"Smile, kids," Mrs. Bates whispered. "Straighten your shoulders. Stand tall."

Step by step, with enormous effort, we managed to get through the crush of human bodies. The courtroom was smaller than I'd imagined, about the size of an average living room, with wooden benches lining either side of a narrow aisle. I had heard someone say the courtroom held only 150 people. It was **filled to overflowing**. I was glad to see that a good number of the **spectators** were our people. Sections of the room were roped off. We were squeezed through the crowd and ushered to one of the areas in front, near the **bailiff**.

Reporters holding their notebooks sat in the jury box and in a small section at the rear of the room. As we took our seats, I noticed the United States and Arkansas flags displayed in the front of the room.

"Niggers stink. The room smells now," a voice called out from somewhere behind us. I turned around to see three white ladies directly behind me.

Suddenly uniformed soldiers were arriving. I turned my attention away from the woman heckling me as the soldiers paraded down the aisle with military precision. So these were the armed men who were keeping us away from school. These were the leaders of the Arkansas National Guard. Up close, they seemed much less **intimidating**. Some of them were no

....

filled to overflowing completely full of people
spectators people in the audience
bailiff courtroom officer
intimidating scary, frightening

taller than I was.

Several men and one woman, all wearing business suits and carrying briefcases, were talking to the uniformed men. I figured they were the governor's attorneys. I asked where the governor was, expecting him any moment. That's when one of the attorneys told us that an elected official does not have to appear to answer a **summons**. Maybe I would not have the privilege of seeing the governor after all. I had hoped that seeing him in person would help me get over my dislike for him.

Suddenly a whisper of concern made its way through our group. We **were all aware** that Thelma Mothershed had a heart condition, and now, right before our eyes, her lips and fingertips were turning blue. She struggled to catch her breath. All of us focused our attention on her, and instantly I knew it was a mistake. Not only might it alarm her, but our behavior could also alert school officials to her **failing health**. I assumed they had never bothered to check her school records; otherwise they might have stopped her going to the integration.

"Shhhh. Thelma will be just fine. Sit up straight. Think about what you'll say if you're called to testify." Mrs. Bates relieved our tension as she moved to sit beside Thelma.

"All rise. The Honorable Judge Ronald Davies **presiding**." The deep voice sounded like a circus ringmaster announcing the next act. I held my breath. I had read so much about him. What would he be like? A very small man wearing a black robe entered and moved swiftly toward the massive desk. His smooth dark hair was parted in the middle, framing his pleasant round face.

....

summons court order to appear before a judge
were all aware knew
failing health illness; medical condition
presiding is judging this case

As he climbed up to the imposing leather chair and settled in, what stood out most of all were his huge eyes peering through thick horn-rimmed glasses. From where I sat, I could see only the top part of his black robe, his round face, and those all-seeing, all-knowing eyes.

The seats were so hard that I was pleased Judge Davies moved things along swiftly, pounding his gavel, **denying motions** presented by the governor's attorneys, all the while speaking sternly. Finally, just before noon, one of the attorneys, Tom Harper, speaking for Governor Faubus, asked if preliminary matters were taken care of.

"Well," the judge growled, "I haven't gotten the late mail, but I think so."

Continuing in a matter-of-fact tone, Harper then asked Judge Davies to dismiss the case because it involved constitutional issues that required a three-judge panel. Judge Davies ruled that the case would continue. In response to that ruling, Harper said, "May we be excused?"

Judge Davies spoke emphatically: "You are excused, gentlemen, but you understand that this **is a moot question**. The hearing will proceed."

Harper began reading a statement. "The position of Governor Faubus and the military officials of the state is that the governor and the state will not **concede** that the U.S. Court or anyone else can question the authority of the governor to exercise his judgment in **administering the affairs of** state, and since he does not concede this responsibility, we will not

....

denying motions saying no to the legal requests

is a moot question will not affect the case

concede agree

administering the affairs of making decisions for the

proceed further in this action."

To my amazement, Harper led the way as several men and one woman gathered their papers and followed him out the door. "Is this a protest?" someone asked. Reporters ran for the door like corralled horses through an open gate. I thought they'd hurt themselves. The judge pounded the gavel.

The attorneys for the Department of Justice called themselves *amicus curiae*, saying they were prepared to offer more than one hundred witnesses to support the order for integration. Word was whispered down our line that *amicus curiae* meant "friend of the court." But surely no real friend would keep us sitting on those hard seats long enough for a hundred people to testify. My heart sank as we nine **eyeballed** one another with grim expressions.

"We'll be too old for high school if we have to listen to all those people," I whispered aloud. To my delight, the judge announced the hundred witnesses would not begin until after lunch.

In order to get to our lunch, we walked through a **gauntlet** of hot flashing lights and squeezed past people shouting questions. Once outside, we encountered the problem that had always **plagued** our people in Little Rock. There were no restaurants that would serve us, at least no **decent** ones.

The mighty Thurgood Marshall was forced to join us in a greasy joint that served wilted lettuce on overcooked hamburgers in the shabby section of our neighborhood known as Ninth Street. As he ate, he answered our questions.

··

eyeballed looked at
gauntlet line, crowd
plagued been a problem for
decent good

More than anything he seemed to be astonished that the governor's attorneys had walked out of the room so suddenly. "It must have been their plan all along," he said.

That afternoon the parade of witnesses presented by the Justice Department made one major point. They said the threat of violence due to integration was not sufficient for the governor to have called out troops.

School Superintendent Virgil Blossom testified for a long time about the details of the school board's plan for integration, which had taken two years and two hundred meetings to devise.

"How were these nine students chosen?"

"The Negroes were selected on the basis of **scholarship**, personal conduct, and health. We picked those who had the mental ability to do the job and had used it," Blossom answered.

For just a moment, I **fretted** they would discover Thelma's secret heart problem. But the fact was, they had never had us examined by a doctor and there was no talk of doing so.

Then it was time to present our case. First to testify from our group was Ernest Green. He wanted to go to Central, he said, because it was closer to his home and would save time and money. He was asked whether he offered any assault against the troops. "No, sir, I didn't," he said with a broad smile.

Next, Elizabeth Eckford testified. She did not complain about the life-threatening mob that had **traumatized** her. She sat erect, speaking calmly, saying that a few white people lived not far from her house, yet there had been no racial **disputes**.

....

scholarship school performance; their grades
fretted worried
traumatized frightened, upset
disputes disagreements, fights

I was relieved when the attorney said that there would be no need for the rest of us to testify.

The attorneys for the United States made repeated references to the May 1954 decision. I had to stop listening. The very mention of that decision always made me sad. It brought back the face of the angry white man who had chased me down that day. Panic-filled recollections flooded my mind, blotting out the courtroom proceedings.

"Melba! Melba!" Minnijean was tugging at my arm. The others were excited.

The judge was announcing his decision, saying that the governor had **"thwarted"** the court-approved plan of integration by **means of** National Guard troops. The judge's voice was deep, his tone emphatic, as he said, "There is no real evidence here that we shouldn't proceed with the court-ordered integration of Central High School. The order is so entered." He pounded the gavel, stood, and walked out of the room.

"Oh, damn nigger-loving judge!" someone shouted, using all those words that Grandma said **would lead a body to hell**.

Mrs. Bates told us to remain seated until everyone else left the room. I sat very still for a long moment as everybody around me began moving. So, God, you really do want me to go back to that school. For a time it seemed as if I were all alone in a silent tunnel, and everyone else was way at the other end. I would always remember that judge and his huge, piercing dark eyes. There must be something wonderful in his heart, I thought. I would remember him in my prayers.

....

"thwarted" stopped, prevented
means of using
would lead a body to hell were bad; were sinful

"Come Monday morning you'll be a **genuine** Central High student. How do you feel about that?" one reporter shouted his question above all others.

"Monday morning," I whispered, "I'm gonna be a Central High student—Monday morning!"

....

genuine real, actual

BEFORE YOU MOVE ON...

1. **Argument** Reread pages 86–87. What was the argument the governor's attorneys used in court?

2. **Summarize** Reread pages 88–89. How did the Justice Department argue for integration?

LOOK AHEAD Read pages 91–113 to find out what happened when Melba entered Central High for the first time.

7

CITY AND STATE POLICE TO BE THERE TODAY; OFFICIALS CONFIDENT. FAUBUS SAYS HE'S HOPING FOR NO **UNREST**; U.S. KEEPING CLOSE EYE ON LITTLE ROCK
—*Arkansas Gazette*, Monday, September 23, 1957

As I read the morning newspaper that Monday, what with all the changes, I thought maybe the headline would read, "Integration Halted Again." At least this time it seemed everybody was expecting us to arrive at Central High School and go inside for classes.

As I walked back to the kitchen, I decided I would begin to **mark off** my days at Central High on the big wall calendar that belonged to Grandma. I longed to see all the cross marks fill the days that would become weeks and then months. I glanced at the month of September and picked the spot where I would put the first cross mark, if I completed the first day. Lord, please let me be strong enough to fill in this day and all the school days that follow, I whispered.

....

UNREST FIGHTING, VIOLENCE
mark off count

91

It was not yet eight o'clock when Mama and I parked at the curb just outside Mrs. Bates's home. I was surprised to see so many people **milling about** the yard. There was double the usual throng of news reporters. Everybody spoke in whispers. I was ushered through the crowd and into the living room, where radio and news reports held everyone's attention.

We nine acknowledged one another with nervous smiles and a very few whispered words. Adults nodded to each other with the kind of glances that seemed to carry secret messages as they periodically looked at their watches. The nervousness grew worse with each passing moment. People were pacing, pretending to smile, sitting a moment, then rising to pace again. After a while, I became one of those people. We were going to be late for school, no doubt—late on the first day. What would everybody think? The phone rang. It was time to be on our way.

Mother Lois looked as though she were **on the brink of tears**. As we **filed** silently out of the house, I waved good-bye to her. I wanted to hug her, but I didn't want everyone to think I was a baby. Other parents milled about, looking as if we were being **carted off** to be hanged. As we started to walk to the cars, they clutched at us as though they weren't completely certain we'd be coming back.

We settled ourselves into two cars. Mrs. Bates was in the first car with four of the nine, and a man introduced as C. C. Mercer. Another NAACP official, Frank Smith, was driving the car I rode in with the remaining four students. We watched the

....

milling about in; crowding
on the brink of tears about to cry
filed walked
carted off taken away

news reporters run to their vehicles and rev their engines. The nonwhite reporters seemed hesitant about getting started. They hovered together. That's when I realized it must be difficult, even dangerous, for our people to **cover** a story like this.

We seemed at first to be driving in circles. Our driver explained that the police advised we not take the usual route because segregationists might **lie in wait for** us. I looked at my watch. It was after eight-thirty. We'd be very late arriving— even later than I had feared.

Central High was located on Park Street, stretching a two-block distance between Fourteenth and Sixteenth streets. But the route we took confused my sense of direction. I was surprised when suddenly we pulled up to the side entrance at Sixteenth Street, just beyond Park. Amid noise and confusion, the driver urged us to get out quickly. The white hand of a uniformed officer reached out toward the car, opening the door and pulling me toward him as his urgent voice ordered us to hurry. The roar coming from the front of the building made me glance to my right. Only a half block away, I saw hundreds of white people, their bodies in motion, their mouths wide open as they shouted their anger.

"The niggers! Keep the niggers out!" The shouts came closer. The roar swelled, as though their **frenzy had been fired up** by something. It took a moment to **digest the fact** that it was the sight of us.

Hustled along, we walked up the few concrete stairs, through the heavy double doors that led inside the school, and then up a

....

cover work on; report
lie in wait for be waiting to attack
frenzy had been fired up anger was increased
digest the fact understand, realize

few more stairs. It was like entering a darkened movie theater—amid the rush of a crowd eager to get seated before the picture begins. I was barely able to see where we were rushing to. There were blurred images all around me as we moved up more stairs. The sounds of footsteps, ugly words, insulting shouts, and whispered commands formed an echoing **clamor**.

"Niggers, niggers, the niggers are in." They were talking about me. The shouting wouldn't stop; it got louder as more joined in.

"They're in here! Oh, God, the niggers are in here!" one girl shouted, running ahead of us down the hallway.

"They got in. I smell something. . . ."

"You niggers better turn around and go home."

I was racing to keep pace with a woman who shouted orders over her shoulders to us. Nobody had yet told us she was someone we could trust, someone we should be following. I tried to move among the angry voices, blinking, struggling to accustom my eyes to the very dim light. The unfamiliar surroundings reminded me of the inside of a museum—marble floors and stone walls and long winding hallways that seemed to go on forever. It was a huge, **cavernous** building, the largest I'd ever been in. Breathless, I made my legs carry me quickly past angry white faces, **dodging** fists that struck out at me.

"The principal's office is this way," whispered a petite woman with dark hair and glasses. "Hurry, now, hurry." I was walking as fast as I could. Then we were shoved into an office where there was more light. Directly in front of us, behind

....

clamor noise
cavernous open and very wide
dodging avoiding; moving away from

a long counter, a row of white people, mostly women, stood staring at us as though **we were the world's eighth wonder**.

In the daylight, I recognized Mrs. Huckaby, Central High's vice-principal for girls, who had been present at several of our earlier meetings with the school board.

"This is Jess Matthews, the principal," she said. "You remember him."

No, I didn't remember. He peered at us with an acknowledging frown and nod, then quickly walked away.

"Here are your class schedules and homeroom assignments. Wait for your guides," Mrs. Huckaby said.

That's when I noticed that just beyond the glass panels in the upper part of the door that led to the office clusters of students stood glaring at us. One boy opened the door and walked in, yelling, "You're not gonna let those niggers stay in here, are you?"

All at once Thelma Mothershed slumped down on the wooden bench just inside the door of the office. Mrs. Huckaby hustled the boy out and turned her attention to Thelma, as we all did. She was pale, her lips and fingertips blue. Breathless as she was, she mustered a faint smile and tried to **reassure us**.

None of us wanted to leave her there with those white strangers, but Mrs. Huckaby seemed to be a **take-charge** person who would look after her. She ushered us out, saying we had to go. Just for an instant, I worried about how Thelma's parents would get through the huge crowd outside to pick her up if she were really ill.

---

we were the world's eighth wonder they had never seen an African American before

reassure us make us believe she was okay

take-charge responsible, confident

Three thirty-nine, that was the number of the homeroom on my card; I was assigned to the third floor. We quickly compared notes. Each of us was assigned to a different homeroom.

"Why can't any of us be in the same homeroom or take classes together?" I asked. From behind the long desk, a man spoke in an unkind booming voice. "You wanted integration . . . you got integration."

I turned to see **the hallway swallow up my friends**. None of us had an opportunity to say a real good-bye or make plans to meet. I was alone, in a daze, following a muscular, stocky white woman with closely cropped straight black hair. Up the stairs I went, squeezing my way past those who first blocked my path and then shouted hurtful words at me. "Frightened" did not describe my state; I had moved on to terrified. My body was numb. I was only aware of my head and thoughts and visions.

I had fantasized about how wonderful it would be to get inside the huge beautiful castle I knew as Central High School. But the reality was so much bigger, darker, and more **treacherous** than I had imagined. I could easily get lost among its spiral staircases. The angry voices shouting at me made it all the more difficult to find my way through these unfamiliar surroundings. I was panic-stricken at the thought of losing sight of my guide. I ran to keep up with her.

"Move it, girlie," she called back at me.

"Pheeew!" one boy said, backing away from me. Others stopped and joined in his **ridicule**. For an instant I stood paralyzed.

....

the hallway swallow up my friends my friends leaving
treacherous dangerous, unsafe
"Pheeew!" "You smell bad!"
ridicule insults; name-calling

I had long dreamed of entering Central High. I could not
have imagined what that privilege could cost me.
(*Bettmann/Corbis*)

Me, at fifteen, the year I entered the battlefield of Little Rock Central High.
(*Author collection*)

My mother, Lois Peyton Pattillo, gave me strength and kept me focused on my goal.
(*Author collection*)

Without my grandmother, India Anette Peyton, I would not have survived my year at Central. (*Author collection*)

Almost every day I came home from Central, my brother, Conrad, would meet me on his bike and tell me: "Sis, remember, I like you," or, "You're not so bad for a big sis." He was always a support. (*Author collection*)

On the day I watched Elizabeth Eckford being brave in the face of the mob, I felt both helpless and vulnerable.
(*Bettmann/Corbis*)

I will always be grateful to the men of the 101st Airborne, who did their personal best to protect us from attacks.
(*George Silk/Time and Life Pictures/Getty Images*)

The NAACP chief counsel, Thurgood Marshall, visited with us on the steps of the Supreme Court. From left to right: me; Jefferson Thomas; Gloria Ray; Mrs. C. Bates, president of the NAACP in Little Rock; Thurgood Marshall; Carlotta Walls; Minnijean Brown; and Elizabeth Eckford.
(*Bettmann/Corbis*)

Our family home, which had always been my sanctuary, became a prison during the year of integration.
(*Author collection*)

Thelma Mothershed sits on the arm of my chair as we do our Central High homework. (*AP/Wide World Photos*)

Sometimes we met at the home of Little Rock's NAACP president to connect with the soldiers who guarded us. She, like other community activists and especially our parents, did her best to support us. But none of them could go into those hostile halls and classrooms day after day with us. Only we nine shared the horrors of being inside Central High.
(*Thomas McAvoy/Time and Life Pictures/Getty Images*)

We nine students involved in the integration of Central High School became a closely knit family with one goal—to survive. Front row: Thelma Mothershed, Elizabeth Eckford, and me. Back row: Jefferson Thomas, Ernest Green, Minnijean Brown, Carlotta Walls, Terrence Roberts, and Gloria Ray.
(*UPI/Bettmann Newsphotos*)

"Don't stop!" the woman commanded. Her words **snapped me into action**. I scuffled to move behind her. Suddenly I felt it—the sting of a hand slapping the side of my cheek, and then warm, slimy saliva on my face, dropping to the collar of my blouse.

A woman stood toe-to-toe with me, not moving. "Nigger!" she shouted in my face again and again. She appeared to be a little older than my mother. Her face was distorted by rage. "Nigger bitch. Why don't you go home?" she lashed out at me. "Next thing, you'll want to marry one of our children." A⊤ HA

Marry, I thought, as I darted around her. I wasn't even allowed to go on a real date. Grandma wouldn't let me marry. Besides, why would I choose to marry one of those mean Little Rock white people? My **temples throbbed**, my cheek stung, the spit was still on my face. It was the first time I had ever been spat upon. I felt hurt, embarrassed. I wondered if I'd catch her germs. Before I could wipe it off, my guide's harsh command summoned me to move.

"Get going. Now. Do you hear me? Move! Now!" I brushed the saliva off my nose with my hand.

As I entered the classroom, **a hush fell over the students**. The guide pointed me to an empty seat, and I walked toward it. Students sitting nearby quickly gathered their books and moved away. I sat down, surrounded by empty seats, feeling unbearably self-conscious. Still, I was relieved to be off my feet. I was **disoriented**, as though my world were blurred and leaning to the left, like a photograph snapped from a twisted angle and

....

snapped me into action made me walk faster
temples throbbed head hurt
a hush fell over the students everyone became silent
disoriented confused

out of focus. A middle-aged woman, whom I assumed to be the teacher, ignored me.

"Open your book to page twelve," she said, without allowing her eyes to acknowledge me.

"Are you gonna let that nigger coon sit in our class?" a boy shouted as he glared at me. I waited for the teacher to say or do something.

"Now, class, if you've done the homework, then you know—" A loud voice cut her off, shouting, "We can **kick the crap out of** this nigger." The heckler continued. "Look, it's twenty of us and one of her. They ain't nothing but animals."

Again, I waited for the teacher to speak up, but she said nothing. Some of the students **snickered**. The boy took his seat, but he kept shouting ugly words at me throughout the rest of the class. My heart was weeping, but I squeezed back the tears. I squared my shoulders and tried to remember what Grandma had said: "God loves you, child; no matter what, he sees you as his precious idea."

Walking the gauntlet to my next class was even more **harrowing**. I had to go out behind the school, through the girls' dressing room, down a long concrete walkway, and onto the playing field.

"You'd better watch yourself," the guide warned as we moved at high speed through the hostile students. As we went outside to the walkway in the back of the school, I could hear the roar of the crowd in front of the school. It was even **more deafening** than the jeers immediately around me.

....

kick the crap out of beat up
snickered laughed
harrowing frightening
more deafening louder

On the playing field, groups of girls were tossing a volleyball. The teacher appeared to be a no-nonsense person. With a pleasant smile, she pointed me to a spot near the net and warned the other girls not to bother me.

"Let's keep the game going, girls," she said in a **matter-of-fact** way. The girls paused for a moment, looked at one another, looked at me, and then began tossing the ball back and forth. For just one instant, I was actually concerned about whether or not I could hit the ball and score. It took me a moment to realize it was whizzing awfully close to my head. I ducked, but they hit me real hard, shouting and cheering as they found their target. RP

And even as I was struggling to escape their cruelty, I was at the same time more terrified by the sound of the angry crowd in the distance. It must be enormous, I thought. How would the police keep them back?

"Get inside, Melba. Now!" The face of the gym teacher showed both compassion and alarm as she quietly pointed to a group of women some distance away, jumping over the rear fence as they shouted **obscenities** at me. "Hurry!"

I started to run for my life.

"Nigger . . . nigger . . ." one woman cried, **hot on my heels**. "Get the nigger." Three of them had broken away from the **pack** and were gaining on me. I was running at top speed when someone stuck out a foot and tripped me. I fell face forward, cutting my knee and elbow. Several girls moved closer, and for an instant I hoped they were drawing near to extend a hand

....

matter-of-fact simple, calm

obscenities mean words

hot on my heels chasing me

pack rest of the group

and ask me if I needed help. "The nigger is down," one shouted. "She's bleeding. What do you know. Niggers bleed red blood. Let's kick the nigger." I saw the foot coming my way and grabbed it before it got to my face. I twisted it at the ankle like I'd seen them do at the wrestling match. The girl fell backward.

As I scrambled to my feet, I looked back to see the brigade of attacking mothers within striking distance, shouting about how they weren't going to have me in school with their kids. ⓔ

I ran up the stairs, hoping I could find my way back to the office. With the mothers close on my heels, shouting their threats, the twisted maze of the hallway seemed even more **menacing**. I felt I could have gotten lost forever as I struggled to find the door that led to the office and safety, opening first one, then another. I raced through a **honeycomb** of locker rooms and dead-end hallways.

After several minutes of opening the wrong doors and bumping into people who hit me or called me names, I was in tears, ready to give up, paralyzed by my fear. Suddenly Grandma's voice came into my head: "God never loses one of his flock." Shepherd, show me how to go, I said. I stood still and repeated those words over and over again until I **gained some composure**. I wiped my eyes, and then I saw blood running down my leg and onto my saddle shoe. It was too much! I pressed my thumb to the wounded area to try to stop the bleeding.

"I've been looking for you." The stocky guide's voice was angry, but I was so glad to see her I almost forgot **myself** and

....

menacing scary, terrifying
honeycomb maze
gained some composure became calmer
myself that I was not her friend

reached to hug her. "And just where do you think you are going? You are only supposed to travel through the school with me." She looked at my leg but said nothing, then looked away.

"Yes, ma'am, but—"

"But nothing. Let's go to **shorthand class**." She didn't know it, but she was the answer to my prayer. I looked over my shoulder to see the group of mothers standing still, obviously unwilling to come after me with a school official at my side. I choked back tears and speeded my steps.

"Hello, honey, welcome. We're just beginning. I'm Mrs. Pickwick." The warm voice of the tiny dark-haired woman comforted me. Although she was petite, I quickly discovered that my shorthand teacher was definitely not one to **tolerate any hanky-panky**. When students moved away from me, hurling insults, she gave them a stern reprimand. "If you move, you move to the office and see the principal," she said without so much as a hint of compromise in her voice.

As I headed for the last row of empty seats by the window, she called out to me, "Melba, stay away from the window." Her voice was sympathetic, as though she really cared what happened to me. As I turned back to follow her orders, I caught a glimpse of the crowd across the street from the front of the school. I was so **transfixed** by the sight, I couldn't move. The ocean of people stretched farther than I could see—waves of people **ebbing and flowing**, shoving the sawhorses and the policemen who were trying to keep them in place. There were lots of uniformed policemen, but the crowd must have

....

shorthand class note-taking class
tolerate any hanky-panky allow any bad behavior
transfixed amazed, fascinated
ebbing and flowing moving and pushing

outnumbered them **a hundredfold**. Every now and then, three or four people broke through and dashed across the street toward the front of the school. The police would run after them.

"Melba, please take your seat."

Slowly, reluctantly, I turned away and stumbled to my seat. As I sat there, trying to focus on the shorthand book before me, I could hear some of the things the crowd was shouting. "Get the niggers," and "Two, four, six, eight, we ain't gonna integrate."

Although I could not erase the images or the sounds of those people outside, somehow Mrs. Pickwick was so sincere and determined to be as normal as possible that I actually listened to what she had to say about shorthand. I even managed to draw several shorthand characters on my tablet as the noise got louder and louder. I looked up from my notes to see my guide entering the door. She wore a frown and was red-faced and perspiring. Something was awfully wrong. **It was written all over her face.**

"Come with me now. To the principal's office," she called out nervously. This time she collected my books and shoved them into my arms. I walked even faster than before. We were almost running. "Don't stop for anything," she shouted at me over the noise.

As I followed her through an inner office past very official-looking white men, I was alarmed by the anxious expressions on their faces. I was led to **an adjoining anteroom**—a smaller office, where some of the eight had gathered. Two of the girls

....

a hundredfold by hundreds of people
It was written all over her face. I could see she was scared.
an adjoining anteroom a nearby room

were crying. I stood near the door, which was ajar enough so that although I could not see who was speaking, I could hear much of the men's conversations. I heard their frantic tone of voice, heard them say the mob was out of control, that they would have to call for help. "What are we gonna do about the nigger children?" asked one.

"The crowd is moving fast. They've broken the barricades. These kids are trapped in here."

"Good Lord, you're right," another voice said. "We may have to let the mob have one of these kids, so's we can distract them long enough to get the others out."

"Let one of those kids **hang**? How's that gonna look? Niggers or not, they're children, and we got a job to do."

Hang one of us? They were talking about hanging one of my friends, or maybe even me. My knees were shaking so badly I thought I would fall over. I held my breath, trying not to make any noise. The two men discussing our **fate** were just on the other side of the door. I turned my back to the partially opened door, at the same time moving closer to it so I could hear more.

A man's voice said, "They're children. What'll we do, have them **draw straws** to see which one gets a rope around their neck?"

"It may be the only way out. There must be a thousand people out there, armed and coming this way."

"Some of these patrolmen are **throwing down their badges**," another breathless voice said. "We gotta get them out of here."

....

hang be killed

fate lives, futures

draw straws play a game of luck

throwing down their badges quitting their jobs

I heard footsteps coming closer. I moved to the center of the room, closer to where my friends stood surrounding Thelma, who sat on her haunches.

A tall, raw-boned, dark-haired man came toward us. "I'm Gene Smith, Assistant Chief of the Little Rock Police Department." He spoke in a calm tone. "It's time for you to leave for today. Come with me now." Right away, I had a good feeling about him because of the way he introduced himself and **took charge**. He urged us to move faster, acting as though **it mattered to him** whether or not we got out. "It's eleven-thirty. I want you out of here before noon."

Gene Smith. His was the voice I had heard in the next room, saying he would rather get all of us out than hang one to save the others. I decided to forever remember this man in my prayers. I scrambled to keep up with the others as we moved at a quick pace toward the Fourteenth Street side of Central High. It was almost a block away, but suddenly Smith and the other men turned from the main hallway and began descending stairs into **passageways** that became more and more dim.

What if they were going to kill us? I didn't really know these men, yet I had no choice but to trust them. I focused on speeding down the narrow concrete passageway, down the stairs into a dark cellar, where one of the men walking ahead of us switched on a flashlight. We were inside some kind of basement garage. In the distance was a huge door that appeared to lift upward with chain pulleys. It resembled a loading dock of some kind. Two cars were sitting with engines running, lights on,

....

took charge was in control
it mattered to him he cared
passageways hallways

hoods pointing toward the door.

"Hurry, now . . . get in," Smith said as he held open one of the doors. I looked at the others getting into the second car. Thelma, Minnijean, and Ernie were in the car with me. A white man sat behind the wheel. He had an absolutely terrified expression on his face.

"Roll your windows up, lock your doors, keep your faces away from the windows. Put your heads down when we start to move." He hunched over to secure something on the floor, and that's when I saw the gun strapped to his side in a leather **holster**.

Smith leaned down to talk through the open window to the driver. "Move fast and don't stop no matter what." Then he looked at us and said, "Listen to your driver's instructions and do exactly what he says. **Your lives depend on it**." RP

We were surrounded by white men in suits speaking in frightened tones. Their expressions told me we were in the kind of trouble I hadn't even imagined before. The enormous roaring sound coming from the crowd just beyond the door made me wonder whether or not they had waited too long to get us into these cars. Just for one instant I tried to imagine what would happen if the mob got hold of us.

"Now!" Smith shouted. **"Let 'er roll."**

The driver shifted gears and gunned the engine as I crouched down in the backseat. Suddenly I heard the loud sound of what must have been a heavy chain dragging. The basement door was opening, letting streaks of sunlight in.

··

holster belt

Your lives depend on it. You must do what he says if you do not want to get killed.

"Let 'er roll." "Go!"

I scooted farther down in my seat, hiding my face. But I decided I had to keep my eyes open. I wanted to know what was happening to me. At least that way I'd know what to pray for.

I felt the car surge ahead. We were climbing upward, out of the basement toward bright sunlight. I could hear the tires spin onto a gravel driveway just beyond the door. The car **gained momentum**, lunging forward. As the full light of day crept into the windows, the deafening noise of the mob **engulfed** us.

"Get the niggers! Hang those niggers! Stop those cars," I heard somebody shout. Then I saw wave after wave of white faces, angry white faces, everywhere. Their mouths were open shouting threats. Clusters of white hands with fingers extended seemed for a moment to envelop us, clutching, grabbing at us. Some of the faces were moving along with us, coming closer to the car windows.

"Hold on and keep your heads down," the driver shouted. I heard the engine grind and felt us go faster. The people running beside us **accelerated their pace, hurling** rocks and sticks at the car.

That's when the car really began moving fast, faster than I'd ever ridden before. Finally, there were fewer hands and faces on the car windows, and the noises subsided. I took a deep breath.

"You'all can sit up now. But **keep an eye out**." I could see that the others in the car behind us were safe. We were mostly silent on our journey, craning our necks, keeping watch in every direction. RP Ⓔ

"Thank you for the ride home," I said to the driver as I

------

gained momentum drove faster

engulfed surrounded

accelerated their pace, hurling ran faster, throwing

keep an eye out be careful and watch for others

climbed out of the car. He cast a pleasant but impatient glance my way. I wanted to say, "Thanks for risking your life to save mine," but I didn't know how it would sound to the others. It was an awkward moment with a stranger, a decent white man.

"Get in the house now—go," he said, pausing for an instant, then gunning his engine and pulling away. I waved good-bye to my friends. Standing at the curb for a moment, I peered after the car as it drove away, wondering if he would get into trouble with the segregationists when they found out he was the one who rescued us from the mob. He was the second white man I would pray for God to protect.

I turned to see that some of my neighbors had gathered, a few sitting in our lawn chairs, a few standing around talking. I wondered what they were doing there. Then Grandma India rushed out the front door, her arms open to receive me.

"Thank God you're safe. Your mama is on her way home."

She was shoving me, both her hands at my back, not letting me pause to say hello to the **alarmed** neighbors who kept asking if I was all right.

"Now you've had your lesson. You don't have to go back to that awful school anymore," our neighbor Mrs. Floyd said as Grandma ushered me past her.

I settled down on the couch in front of the television with the radio blasting loud from the hallway. I sipped the Grapette soda Grandma had given me and thought about what the mob might have done to us. I worried that they would come looking for us at our homes.

....

alarmed frightened, upset

Although we had left shortly after noon, **word came** that the mob continued its rampage. Even after the Central High School registrar came out to announce on a microphone that we had been removed, not everyone believed her. Instead, they surged forward, threatening to **overrun** the barricades and the police, demanding to see for themselves that only white students remained. A police official convinced them to send representatives inside the school to check. When three women returned to report we were not there, the mob cheered but continued the siege.

Armed with guns, ropes, and clubs, the report said, they surged toward the school, in the doors and through the halls, dancing and shouting, "Two, four, six, eight, we ain't gonna integrate."

"Melba, where's Melba? Is she all right?" Mother Lois came rushing into the living room, **disheveled and frantic**.

"I'm fine, Mama." I stood to embrace her.

"We've made a mistake. You're definitely not going back to that school."

"What's that on your knee?" Grandma India asked.

"I fell." I decided I didn't need to add to Mother's nervousness. I would wait until she calmed down to explain **the details of my day**.

"I heard they passed the hat and collected a hundred and forty dollars to encourage those policemen to abandon their duties," Grandma added.

"You must have been scared to death. I'm sorry," Mother said.

....

word came we heard

overrun knock down

disheveled and frantic looking very worried and panicked

the details of my day everything that had happened

We all listened as the newscast continued airing sounds of the angry mob taking over the school. I discovered that one reason we were able to slip into the school that morning was that the mob had been **preoccupied** chasing and beating three black reporters, James Hicks, Alex Wilson, and Moses Newsom, whom they had accused of purposely distracting the crowd in order to allow us time to get in the side door. Mr. Wilson was hit on the head with a brick, and even as he lay wounded on the ground, they continued to kick and beat him.

The mob had then turned to beat up white reporters. Several members of the *Life* magazine staff were beaten. Other newspeople and out-of-towners were chased and beaten until they reached police lines. Even after they were inside police cars, **they were showered with rocks**.

A concerned and flustered Conrad rushed into the house to greet me. His friend Clark had told him I was dead. In order to settle him down, Grandma busied him with helping her fix lunch. I **remained glued** to the news, **mulling over** whether or not I should tell them what really happened to me that day. I decided it would only make things worse, and maybe it would make them decide I could never go back to the integration.

Later on we got hold of a copy of the evening newspaper, the *Arkansas Democrat*. The paper was filled with pictures of the crowd and the police trying desperately to control it. Only by looking at those pictures did I begin to understand the real danger of that mob.

In my diary I wrote:

....

preoccupied busy
they were showered with rocks rocks were thrown at them
remained glued could not stop listening
mulling over thinking about; considering

There seems to be no space for me at Central High. I don't want integration to be like the merry-go-round. Please, God, make space for me.

The phone started to ring nonstop with calls from angry strangers spewing hatred and threats. There were also calls from our family and friends inquiring about my safety and warning us that the mob was continuing to search out and beat up people in our neighborhood. One phone call came from a news reporter who asked what I felt about the situation. Before Mother or Grandma caught on to what I was doing, I told him. He complimented me, saying I **was articulate** and asked if I could write. I said yes, and he asked if I would write an article about my first morning at Central. Right there I just jotted down a few notes and started dictating the article to him as it came into my head, the way I wrote letters to God every night in my diary. All the while I was talking to the reporter, I kept our instructions in mind: **Accentuate the positive**— don't complain too much. He said my story would appear in newspapers everywhere just as I had written it because it was on **the Associated Press wire**. Sure enough, the next day I saw it on the front page:

Would you have exchanged places with me and entered Central as I did this morning? I went, and I am glad.

Previous to making actual entrance into Central I had feelings that I'm sure have never been experienced by a child of 15 years.

....

was articulate spoke very well

Accentuate the positive Focus on the good things

the Associated Press wire a national news service that every newspaper could use stories from

Sensations of courage, fear, and challenge haunted me. With the morning, came my definite decision: I must go.   RP E

"The Lord is my strength and my shield; my heart trusted in him, and I am helped." With this verse in mind and a hopeful prayer in my heart I entered the halls of Central High. The spacious halls brought again the school feeling, however the atmosphere was not **conducive to study** but one of uneasiness.

The sea of faces represented no special personality to me. Although some were kind, many showed **contempt**, especially some boys gathered in the halls.

I was beginning to believe that the long hard fight was over, that finally this American way of life was going to pay off. As I walked through the halls alone it seemed as if I were lost on an island, an island of strange people, having no way of communicating with them. I longed to tell them, "I won't hurt you, honest, give me a chance, come on. How about it? I'm an average teenager, just like yourself, with the same **aspirations and heartaches**." But it was useless, only a few facial expressions told me I had **gotten through**.

Each time as I was about to give up, exhausted from the jeers and insulting remarks, some kind face would come up and say: "I want you here" or "You're pretty" or "Won't you stay and fight it out?"

This above all made all the "Go home, nigger" and "I'm gonna get you before the day is over" fade into the background.

There were a few trying experiences such as being blocked from passage to class by a few rough, tough-looking

....

conducive to study one of learning
contempt hatred, dislike
aspirations and heartaches dreams and disappointments
gotten through been understood

sideburners, boys who I'm sure if separated would not attack a mouse. Then, there were the three women who jumped the fence and attempted to "get me." *RD*

A favorite activity of the kids was to form a group in a circle and scream: "Two, four, six, eight, we ain't gonna integrate." I know of no physical injury to any of the nine students. I was slapped by one girl. I turned and said "Thank you" and continued on my journey to class.

I did not realize the size or the intentions of the crowd outside until I was told for my safety I had to leave Central High. This hurt me deeper than I can ever express. I'm glad I went, Oh, so glad I went, for now I know without out-of-school interference integration is possible in Little Rock, Arkansas.

When I finished the article I realized it was not the whole truth but a version that wouldn't **jeopardize** the integration. If I had told what really happened, one of the officials might say we couldn't go back. I composed the story in a way that would make my day sound okay. Maybe in a few days, if I remained patient and prayed, it would really be that way—white students would welcome me and smile and treat me like an ordinary human being.

All that evening we continued **our vigilance on the couch in front of the television**. From his Sea Island, Georgia, retreat, Governor Faubus urged our leaders and school officials to allow **a cooling-off period** before resuming integration.

....

jeopardize risk; put in danger

our vigilance on the couch in front of the television carefully watching the news on television

a cooling-off period time for people to calm down

President Eisenhower issued a warning statement:

I will use the full power of the United States, including whatever force may be necessary, to prevent **any obstruction of the law** and to **carry out** the orders of the Federal Court.

But even after the President's warning, early Tuesday morning the mob gathered in front of Central High and continued their rampaging.

....

any obstruction of the law anyone or anything from trying to stop the integration
carry out complete, fulfill

BEFORE YOU MOVE ON...

1. **Paraphrase** Reread page 96. What did the man mean when he told Melba, "you wanted integration . . . you got integration"?

2. **Viewing** Look at the pictures in this chapter. How do they help you to understand integration?

LOOK AHEAD Read pages 114–131 to find out who sent Melba a message.

8

"Governor Faubus didn't ask for federal troops, but **they're up in his face anyhow,**" Grandma said as we sat watching the arrival of the 101st Airborne Division early Tuesday evening. We were transfixed as we listened to newsmen describe the power of that very special military unit.

> Fifty-two planeloads—C123's and C130's have brought 1200 battle-equipped paratroopers to Little Rock to see that integration is carried out at Central High School without further violence.

For the first time ever, Grandma placed dinner on trays in front of the television so we could hear President Eisenhower speak to the nation. "Let's **put things into perspective**. He is our President, and he happens to be talking about us. The whole world's watching, why shouldn't we," she said.

Speaking from the White House, President Eisenhower said he sent troops because "**Mob rule** in Little Rock **menaces** the very safety of the United States and the free world."

....

they're up in his face anyhow they came here anyway
put things into perspective think about this logically
Mob rule Groups of angry whites taking control
menaces threatens; puts at risk

Later Governor Faubus came on television to give what one reporter described as a pleading speech. "We are now **an occupied territory**. In the name of God, whom we all revere, in the name of liberty we hold so dear, in the name of decency which we all cherish, what's happening in America?"

"I can help you figure this out, Mr. Faubus," Mother Lois shouted at the screen. "The President has **called your bluff**."

Later that night as my head was swimming with news reports and questions about whether or not to go back to Central High, I wrote in my diary:

> *Everything in my life is so new. Could I please do some of the old things that I know how to do again. I don't know how to go to school with soldiers. Please show me. . . .*
> *P.S. Please help the soldiers to keep the mobs away from me.*

It was very quiet as I turned out the light. With the 101st in town, we didn't hear as many sirens going off. Later, when I woke up thirsty and went to get water, I found Grandma snoring with the rifle lying across her lap. Maybe she felt safer, too.

I don't know how long I'd been asleep when I was jolted awake. I sat straight up in bed. The doorbell was ringing, and I heard voices on the front porch. Mama was standing over me. She put her hand over my mouth and motioned me to get up. The doorbell kept ringing over and over again. We moved toward the living room.

"Who is it?" Grandma yelled through the door as she peeked

---

an occupied territory no longer a free state
called your bluff decided to take control

through the covered glass inset. "White men. It's white men wearing black hats. What are they doing on our front porch at this time of night?" Grandma said as she picked up the shotgun. Then she shouted through the door again: "**State your business, gentlemen, or I'll be forced to do mine.**" *Bordoiss*

"We're from the Office of the President of the United States; please open your door," they called back. "We have a message from your President."

Grandma opened the door ever so slightly and demanded that they show proof of who they were. They passed their identification through the half-opened door. Mother Lois examined the writing closely and nodded a yes.

"How can we help you?" Grandma lowered the gun to her side, keeping it hidden as she opened the front door a bit more. Mother Lois stood beside her. I thought it was funny as I looked around and noticed we were all wearing our nightgowns and pajamas to greet the messengers from the President of the United States.

"Let your daughter go back to school, and she will be protected," one of the men said, handing Mother Lois an envelope.

The next morning, Wednesday, September 25, at 8 A.M., as we turned the corner near the Bateses' home, I saw them, about fifty uniformed soldiers of the 101st. Some stood tall with their rifles at their sides, while others **manned** the jeeps parked at the curb. Still other troops walked about holding walkie-talkies

---

"State your business, gentlemen, or I'll be forced to do mine." "Tell me why you are here, or I will have to use my gun."

manned sat in

to their ears. As I **drew nearer** to them I was fascinated by their well-shined boots. Grandma had always said that well-kept shoes were the **mark of a disciplined individual**. Their guns were also glistening as though they had been polished, and the creases were sharp in the pant legs of their uniforms.

I had heard all those newsmen say "Screaming Eagle Division of the 101st," but those were just words. I was seeing human beings, flesh-and-blood men with eyes that looked back at me. They resembled the men I'd seen in army pictures on TV and on the movie screen. Their faces were white, their expressions blank.

There were lots of people of both races standing around, talking to one another in whispers. I recognized some of the ministers from our churches. Several of them nodded or smiled at me. I was a little concerned because many people, even those who knew me well, were staring as though I were different from them.

Thelma and Minnijean stood together inspecting the soldiers close up while the other students milled about. I wondered what we were waiting for. I was told there was an assembly at Central with the military **briefing the students**.

Reporters hung from trees, perched on fences, stood on cars, and darted about with their usual urgency. Cameras were flashing on all sides. There was **an eerie hush** over the crowd, not unlike the way I'd seen folks behave outside the home of the deceased just before a funeral.

There were tears in Mother's eyes as she whispered good-bye.

....

drew nearer came closer
mark of a disciplined individual sign of a respectful person
briefing the students telling the students what to expect
an eerie hush a strange quiet

"Make this day the best you can," she said.

"Let's bow our heads for a word of prayer." One of our ministers stepped from among the others and began to say comforting words. I noticed tears were streaming down the faces of many of the adults. I wondered why they were crying just at that moment when I had more hope of staying alive and keeping safe than I had since the integration began.

"Protect these youngsters and bring them home. **Flood the Holy Spirit into the hearts and minds of those who would attack our children.**"

"Yes, Lord," several voices echoed.

One of the soldiers stepped forward and beckoned the driver of a station wagon to move it closer to the driveway. Two jeeps moved forward, one in front of the station wagon, one behind. Guns were mounted on the hoods of the jeeps.

We were already a half hour late for school when we heard the order "Move out," and the leader motioned us to get into the station wagon. As we collected ourselves and walked toward the **caravan**, many of the adults were crying openly. When I turned to wave to Mother Lois, I saw tears streaming down her cheeks. I couldn't go back to comfort her.

Sarge, our driver, was friendly and pleasant. He had a Southern accent, different from ours, different even from the one Arkansas whites had. We rolled away from the curb lined with people waving to us. Mama looked even more distraught. I remembered I hadn't kissed her good-bye.

Our **convoy** moved through streets lined with people on

....

Flood the Holy Spirit into the hearts and minds of those who would attack our children. Let the white people think of God and not hurt these children.

caravan line of cars and jeeps that would guide us to school

convoy group of cars

both sides, who stood as though they were waiting for a parade. A few friendly folks from our community waved as we passed by. Some of the white people looked totally horrified, while others raised their fists to us. Others shouted ugly words.

We pulled up to the front of the school. Groups of soldiers on guard were lined at intervals several feet apart. A group of twenty or more was running **at breakneck speed** up and down the street in front of Central High School, their rifles with bayonets pointed straight ahead. Sarge said they were doing crowd control—keeping the mob away from us.

About twenty soldiers moved toward us, forming an olive-drab square with one end open. I glanced at the faces of my friends. Like me, they appeared to be impressed by the **imposing** sight of military power. There was so much to see, and everything was happening so quickly. We walked through the open end of the square. Erect, rifles at their sides, their faces stern, the soldiers did not make eye contact as they surrounded us in a protective cocoon. After a long moment, the leader motioned us to move forward.

I felt proud and sad at the same time. Proud that I lived in a country that would go this far to bring justice to a Little Rock girl like me, but sad that they had **to go to such great lengths**. Yes, this is the United States, I thought to myself. There is a reason that I salute the flag. If these guys just go with us this first time, everything's going to be okay.

We began moving forward. The eerie silence of that moment would **forever be etched in my memory**. All I could hear was

....

at breakneck speed as fast as they could

imposing intimidating, scary

to go to such great lengths to protect us

forever be etched in my memory never be forgotten

my own heartbeat and the sound of boots clicking on the stone.

Everyone seemed to be moving in slow motion as I peered past the raised **bayonets** of the 101st soldiers. I walked on the concrete path toward the front door of the school, the same path the Arkansas National Guard had blocked us from days before. We approached the stairs, our feet moving in unison to the rhythm of the marching click-clack sound of the Screaming Eagles. Step by step we climbed upward—where none of my people had ever before walked as a student. We stepped up to the front door of Central High School and crossed the threshold into that place where angry segregationist mobs had forbidden us to go.

Once the Screaming Eagles had delivered us safely inside the front door of Central High School, all of us—the soldiers, we nine students, white school officials—were standing absolutely still, as though under a spell. No one seemed to know what to do next.

The commander of the troops spoke a few words, and our military protectors **fell into formation** and marched away. I felt naked without that blanket of safety. A warning alarm surged through my body.

Principal Jess Matthews greeted us with a forced smile on his face and directed us to our classrooms. It was then that I saw the other group of soldiers. They were wearing a different uniform from the combat soldiers outside, but they carried the same **hardware** and had the same **placid expressions**. As the nine of us turned to go our separate ways, one by one a soldier

···

bayonets guns
fell into formation moved into their lines
hardware weapons, guns
placid expressions unemotional faces

followed each of us.

Along the winding hallway, near the door we had entered, I passed several clusters of students who stared at me, whispered obscenities, and pointed. They hurled insults at the soldier as well, but he seemed not to pay attention. My class was more than a block away from the front door, near the Fourteenth Street entry to the school. I saw other 101st soldiers standing at intervals along the hall. I turned back to make sure there really was a soldier following me. He was there, all right. As I approached the classroom, he speeded up, coming closer to me.

"Melba, my name is Danny." He looked me directly in the eye. He was slight of build, about five feet ten inches tall, with dark hair and deep-set brown eyes. "I'll be waiting for you here. We're not allowed to go inside the classrooms. If you need me, **holler.**"

My heart skipped a beat as the classroom door closed behind me. I looked back once more and saw Danny's eyes peering through the square glass inset in the door.

The teacher beckoned me to take a seat near the door, where I was in full view of the soldier. I was one of about twenty students.

"You'all just gonna sit still and let this nigger come in here like this? I'm leaving. Who's coming with me?" A tall dark-haired boy paused for a moment, looking around the room. At first, there was silence, but no one left. I took my seat, hoping to settle down and focus on the classwork. Sunlight flooded into the room through a full **bank** of windows along the far wall.

....

holler yell
My heart skipped a beat I was nervous
bank row, group

It was a beautiful morning. I tried hard to concentrate, **tuning myself in** to what the teacher was saying as she continued her discussion of diagramming sentences.

What a stroke of luck. Mother had played a game with Conrad and me, teaching us diagramming at an early age. It's convenient to have a mom who is an English teacher.

"You ugly niggers think just because you got those army boys following you around you gonna stay here."

I swallowed a sadness lump in the back of my throat. I wondered whether or not I should press the teacher to stop the boy from treating me that way. I decided against it because I thought she must be well aware of what he was doing. Besides, we had been instructed not to make a big deal of reporting things in front of other students, lest we be labeled **tattletales**.

The boy continued his taunting throughout the period. At the end of class, I spoke to the teacher to get a list of back assignments, and during the conversation, I asked if she could do something to calm people down.

"I hope you don't think we're gonna **browbeat** our students to please you'all," she said. I pushed down my anger and walked out.

When I entered Mrs. Pickwick's shorthand class things improved decidedly. It was like being on a peaceful island. She remained ever in control. There were a few whispered nasty remarks but no outbursts. Her no-nonsense attitude didn't leave room for unruly behavior.

En route to the next class, I had to use the rest room. I had

---

tuning myself in listening
tattletales complainers, whiners
browbeat punish; yell at
En route On my way

put it off as long as I could. I had hoped I could put it off until I went home. It was what I dreaded most because the girls' rest rooms were so isolated.

Danny leaned against the wall, across from the bathroom door, quite a distance away. I hurried inside. The students appeared astonished at the sight of me.

"There ain't no sign marked Colored on this door, girl," one of them said as I **whizzed** past.

I couldn't respond or even stop to listen to her. I was desperate to find an empty stall. Once inside, with the door closed, I **felt alarmed at** their whispering and scrambling about, but I couldn't make out exactly what they were saying.

I ran out **like a shot**, pausing only a second to get a few drops of water to clean my hands. That's when I noticed it— written all over the mirror with lipstick was "Nigger, go home."

Later that day I hesitated as the throng of students made its way back up the front staircase. When the bottom of the stairway had cleared, Danny motioned me to move ahead. By then I was anxious to go to the cafeteria. I was looking forward to being with my friends, with people I could talk to and laugh with, but Danny said we had been summoned to the vice-principal's office.

He walked only a few steps behind me as I moved cautiously through the **clogged** hallway, avoiding close contact with hecklers wherever I could. We moved up to the second floor and into the office, where I was met by Carlotta, Thelma, and Mrs. Huckaby, the girls' vice-principal. She insisted on escorting us

....

whizzed moved quickly
felt alarmed at was frightened by
like a shot as fast as I could
clolgged crowded

to the rest room and the cafeteria, and we thanked her.

The four of us walked to the lower level and into a wider hallway, a brightly lit area of what appeared to be a basement corridor leading to the biggest cafeteria I had ever seen.

The cafeteria seemed to be half the size of a football field, filled with long tables. There was a roar of noise from the hundreds of chatting, laughing students and the clang of utensils. The line of people waiting to pick up their food appeared to go on forever. Many of the students in that room turned to stare at us. All at once I caught a glimpse of nonwhite faces—my people serving food behind the counter. I didn't feel the same twinge of painful embarrassment I sometimes felt when I saw my people in **service positions** in public places. Instead, I was thrilled to see them smiling back at me.

The cafeteria line was treacherous, but I survived with my tray of food **intact**. Over lunch, Carlotta, Thelma, and I were joined by a couple of friendly white girls. For a brief moment, we laughed and talked about ordinary things as though it were a typical school day. Indeed, a few white students were trying to **reach out to us**. They explained that many of their friends would stay away because they feared segregationists who warned them against any show of kindness toward us.

After lunch, as I headed for gym class, I had two more reasons to hope integration could work. Amid all the hecklers taunting me, two girls had smiled and waved a welcome. Danny and I **parted company** at the door that led to the girls' dressing room. We agreed to meet after I changed into my gym uniform.

....

service positions jobs where they served white people
intact untouched
reach out to us be friendly
parted company separated

He would wait near the head of the narrow corridor that led to gym class. I was frightened as I looked down at the bandage on my knee from the last time I had walked those isolated corridors to gym class. I got out of there as fast as I could.

I entered the dressing room and changed my clothing, going about my business briskly, even when someone tried to block my way. The stares and name-calling hurt, but I was growing accustomed to coping with it. With surprising speed, I changed into my uniform and was on my way out to meet Danny.

He pointed me toward the concrete stairs that led down to the first-level playing field. Several hundred yards beneath us **on what had been an enormous playing field, there was now a huge city**. Hundreds of olive-drab tents stood in meticulous rows. There were jeeps and larger trucks with tarpaulins. It was **an absolute beehive of activity**. Several soldiers were posted directly below us in the field where my class would be. The sight of pristine lines of marching soldiers going back and forth in the distance calmed my nerves.

When class ended, I played a game with myself. I would earn a world record for getting dressed at the fastest speed known to mankind. When Danny greeted me, he confirmed I had far exceeded his expectations. As he trailed me through an isolated passage to the open hallway, we were confronted by a chorus of chants from sideburners. Copying their hairstyle from James Dean and Elvis, they **fancied** themselves to be "bad boys."

"Hut, one two three, march . . . march company . . . march to the beat of the nigger drum," the choir of boys chanted as

....

on what had been an enormous playing field, there was now a huge city the army was now living on the playing field

an absolute beehive of activity very busy

fancied thought of

we walked past. Suddenly, one of them came up to me and slammed my books out of my hand onto the floor. We were surrounded by **thugs**, many much bigger than Danny.

"Don't move," Danny whispered. "Stand absolutely still." His words stopped me from running for my life. At that moment it was hard to remain still; my knees were shaking as the group closed in on us. All at once, from nowhere, other soldiers appeared and made their presence known by holding on to their nightsticks and moving toward us slowly. I wondered where they had come from so quickly. Then I looked behind me and there were still more, standing against the walls, erect and silent, as though steeled to go into action at any moment. *RP*

Reluctantly, the hooligans dispersed, **leaving a trail of** *E* **insults in their wake**. The soldiers withdrew as quickly and quietly as they had appeared, out of sight in an instant.

There was no harsh greeting or heckling as I entered French class. In fact, some of the students wore pleasant expressions. It took a while to realize they had a different kind of **unwelcome mat** for me. I was excited about French class. Mother Lois spoke fluent French; she often gave Conrad and me lessons over the dinner table. I was anxious to get started because I could see that Central had tape recorders and special headphones, things I hadn't had in my French classes before.

The students spent the entire hour speaking in French about suntanning. I understood the language, and I didn't know what to do as one student spoke in French about not wanting to get too dark "for fear of being taken for a . . . Uh, well, you know, a

....

thugs mean, dangerous boys
leaving a trail of insults in their wake yelling insults at us
unwelcome mat mean plan

nigger." I blinked back tears of disappointment.

A serious headache was overtaking me by the time I headed for study hall with Danny tagging behind. Entering the door was like walking into a zoo with the animals outside their cages. The room was double the size of the largest classroom in my old school. I'd never seen anything like it or imagined in my wildest dreams that an important school like Central could allow such outrageous behavior. Stomping, walking, shouting, sailing paper airplanes through the air, students were milling about as though they were having a wild party. The teacher sat **meekly** behind his desk, a **spectator stripped of the desire or power to** make them behave.

I took five steps into the room, and everybody fell silent, abandoning their activities to glare at me.

"Take that seat over there," the study hall teacher said.

"But I need—" I wanted to ask him for a seat near the door where I could see Danny, but he **cut me off**.

"Did you hear me? I said take the seat over there or see the principal."

The teacher returned to reading his newspaper while the students threw spitballs. They directed only a few at me; mostly they were involved in their own little games. At one point, they started passing notes back and forth. When one was passed to me, I opened it. "Nigger go home," it read. I looked at it without emotion, folded it neatly, and put it aside.

"The helicopters are coming to pick up the nigger," someone shouted. Thank God, I thought. I had lived through the wildest

....

meekly nervously

spectator stripped of the desire or power to person watching who knew he could not

cut me off interrupted me; would not let me speak

hour where nobody did anything major to me, but their threats, **near misses**, and flying paper airplanes and pencils had shattered my nerves. "Helicopters. Home," I whispered. It seemed like a lifetime since I had been home and comfortable and safe. Just then Danny opened the door and beckoned to me. "Let's move out for home!" he said.

The engine of the helicopter roared louder as we descended the stairs. Protected by the mighty power of the Screaming Eagles, we walked to the army staff car waiting at the curb. As I stepped into it, **a wave of peace washed over me**.

"Relax, we're on the move," Sarge, our driver, said as we snuggled down into our seats. The convoy was the same as it had been that morning; in front, the open jeep filled with soldiers, a machine gun mounted on its hood, with a similar vehicle behind us. As we pulled away from Central High, I looked back to see students gathered on the school lawn, staring at us as though they were watching a parade they hadn't known was coming their way. For just one tiny instant, I even felt a **twinge of sympathy** for them.

"You'all have a good day, did you?" Sarge said, making polite conversation. We all gave our different versions of the same answer:

"Good isn't exactly the word to describe my day."

"All right."

"Depends on what you mean by good."

"My mama never told me there'd be days like this one."

That was the beginning of a funny **round-robin** to see

---

near misses attempts

a wave of peace washed over me I felt calm

twinge of sympathy little bit sorry

round-robin game where we all took turns speaking

who could describe his or her experience in the most colorful language. The ride home brought the joyful relief I had awaited all day. At times, our stories halted all laughter as we noticed someone's eyes filled with tears. There were tales of flying books and pencils and words that **pierce the soul**. But there were also descriptions of polite students who volunteered to sit beside us or offered to lend back homework assignments or flashed a warm smile just when we needed it most.

Our **respite** was over all too soon. As we approached Mrs. Bates's home, I saw news reporters. My headache started up again. The cameras began to flash even before Sarge could get the car parked. We said our thank-you's to him and turned to **face the bombardment of** questions as we made our way to Mrs. Bates's front door.

"What was it like inside the school? Were you frightened? How were you treated? Did anybody hit you? Did they call you names? What classes are you taking?" Over and over again the same questions. Then there was one that stuck in my mind and made me tighten my jaw. "Are you going back tomorrow?"

I wasn't ready to think of another tomorrow at Central High. I sat quietly and pondered the question as I glanced out the front window at the few soldiers standing at attention. But they were there for only a brief moment before they climbed into the jeeps and the station wagon and rolled away. And then my attention was quickly brought inside by the rude question being asked.

"Would you like to be white?" I scowled at the reporter,

....

pierce the soul were hateful and hurt us
respite break, rest
face the bombardment of answer the many

and he must have understood my irritation. "Uh, I mean, does all this trouble make you'all wish you were white instead of Negro?" he amended his question. $\in$

"Do you wish you were Negro?" I heard the angry words roll out of my mouth. "I'm proud of who I am. My color is **inconvenient** right now, but it won't always be like this." I'd said what I felt, despite the fear that it would be considered **talking back** to an adult.

"Can you write as well as you can speak?" a slender dark-haired man asked.

"I don't know," I answered.

"Why don't you try it? I'm Stan Opotowiski of the *New York Post*, and this is Ted Posten. Here's my card. I would like you to write what you're thinking, and I'll see to it that it's printed." I looked at them. Posten was the same race as me.

"Yeah, sure, I can try." I took the card from him. I told myself I owed him a favor. If reporters hadn't been covering our story, we might have been hanged. News of our demise would be a **three-line notation buried** on the back page of a white newspaper were it not for the Northern reporters' nosy persistence in getting the facts and **dogging the trail of** segregationists.

"We're off to the Dunbar Community Center for another news conference." I couldn't believe my ears, but off we went—once more answering questions in a more formal setting.

---

inconvenient difficult; a problem
talking back speaking rudely
three-line notation buried story no one would see
dogging the trail of following

As we rode home I looked forward to **shedding my day like soiled clothing**. But the first thing I saw as I rounded the corner to my house was reporters sitting in the green lawn chairs on my front porch, holding cameras and notebooks, and a few neighbors gathered in front of my house talking to them. I can't face them, I thought to myself. But I did—I got through it. I smiled, I said the right things, I pretended to be interested in the questions.

By 9 P.M. I was so tired that I only wanted my pillow and dreams—sweet, happy dreams with no white people and no Central High. The next thing I heard was the song on my radio as the alarm went off, waking me out of a cold, sweaty dream. "Peggy . . . Peggy Sue-ue-ue . . ." Buddy Holly was singing.

I picked up my diary and started to write:

*It's Thursday, September 26, 1957. Now I have a **bodyguard**. I know very well that the President didn't send those soldiers just to protect me but to show support for an idea—the idea that a governor can't ignore federal laws. Still, I feel specially cared about because the guard is there. If he wasn't there, I'd hear more of the voices of those people who say I'm a nigger . . . that I'm not valuable, that I have no right to be alive . . .*

Thank you, Danny.

---

shedding my day like soiled clothing not thinking about integration and school

bodyguard *person who protects me*

BEFORE YOU MOVE ON...

1. **Problem and Solution** Reread pages 116–117. What did the president do to protect the students?

2. **Irony** Reread pages 129–130. The reporter asked Melba if she wished she were white. Why was this ironic?

LOOK AHEAD Read pages 132–149 to find out how dangerous Central High became.

9

Overhead, the helicopter was **engaged in its roaring flutter**.
I relaxed a bit because I was, by the second day, familiar with
the military routine of our ride to Central. I allowed myself to
become hypnotized by the sight of soldiers **executing their
duties**.

I asked Sarge if our escorts in the jeeps felt as odd as we did
about **being propped** up there with those big guns mounted in
front of them just to take us to school.

"Nope," he said. "We do what we're told."

Danny was waiting for me near the front door. We nodded
to each other as I began the long trip up to my homeroom. The
early-morning hecklers were full of energy. One girl walked up
close behind me, getting between Danny and me. I didn't look
back; instead I quickened my pace. She started walking on my
heels, and when I turned to face her, she spit at me. I ducked
and **scampered** out of her way. To keep my focus, I began
saying the Lord's Prayer.

"Hey, Melba, pay attention to what you're doing. Watch out!"
Danny shouted as a group of boys bumped straight into me.

---

engaged in its roaring flutter flying over our cars
executing their duties doing their jobs
being propped sitting
scampered ran

One of them kicked me in the shins so hard I fell to the floor.
A second kick was delivered to my stomach. Danny stood over
me, motioning them to move away. Other soldiers made their
presence known, although they kept their distance. I struggled
to my feet. More white students gathered around and taunted
me, applauding and cheering: "The nigger's down."

"**Stand tall**," Danny whispered. "Let's move out."

"Why didn't you do something?" I asked him.

"I'm here for one thing," he said impatiently. "To keep you
alive. I'm not allowed to get into verbal or physical battles with
these students."

As some of the students continued **their catcalls**, I fought
back tears and headed down the stairs to the principal's office.

"Did any adult **witness this incident**?" the woman clerk
asked in an unsympathetic tone. "I mean, did any teacher see
these people do what you said?"

"Yes, ma'am, the soldiers."

"They don't count. Besides, they can't identify the people
you're **accusing**."

"No. I didn't see any adults other than the soldiers," I
answered, feeling the pain in my shin and my stomach.

"Well, in order to do anything, we need an adult witness."

"Yes, ma'am." Those were the words my mouth said because
that's what I had been told was appropriate to say. But another
part of me wanted to shout at her and ask why she didn't believe
me or care enough to ask whether or not I needed medical help.

"I think you'd better get to class, unless you want us to call

....

Stand tall Stand up and ignore them

their catcalls saying mean things

witness this incident see what happened

accusing saying did this to you

an ambulance," she said in a **sarcastic** tone.

I turned to walk out the door. It had hurt my feelings as much to report the incident to her as to live through it. I could see Danny's face, his expression was blank. But his posture was so erect and his stance so commanding that no one would dare to challenge him. Seeing that made me think about my own posture. I had to appear confident and alert. I squared my shoulders, trying not to show how frightened and timid I really felt. I told myself I had to be like a soldier in battle. I couldn't imagine a 101st trooper crying or **moping** when he got hurt.

During the rest of the day, I forced myself to endure annoying little pranks that distracted me and made me nervous but did not really hurt me. After the ride home in the convoy with a fun game of **verbal Ping-Pong** with my friends, the usual group of news reporters once again greeted us at Mrs. Bates's house. That night I wrote in my diary:

> *It's hard being with Little Rock white people. I don't know if I can do this integration thing forever. It feels like this is something people do for only a little while. I want to run away now. I want a happy day.*

The next morning, after a full night's sleep, I felt fresh and new, and the ride with Sarge and the others was a **real tonic** to start my day.

"Smile, it's Friday," Danny said, greeting me at the front door of the school.

....

sarcastic hurtful, unfriendly
moping feeling sorry for himself
verbal Ping-Pong discussing what had happened at school
real tonic good way

Fewer soldiers accompanied us up the front stairs. Their absence meant the defiant chants and hateful words grew much louder. When I stepped inside the school, the soldiers were not as visible as they had been the day before, but I thanked God that they were still there.

"I'm gonna be in the background today. They're trying to figure **how you'all will get along** without us being up real close," Danny said.

I nodded to him as though I felt okay with his announcement. I wanted to say, "Please, please don't leave my side," but I didn't. I felt myself beginning to rely on him, but I didn't know what else to do. I had never before felt such fear. It was an unfamiliar position—me, counting on a white man to defend me against other white people determined to hurt me. And yet I was resigning myself to the fact that, for the moment, I had no choice but to depend on Danny, and God.

As with any high school on Friday, the anticipation of the weekend brought excitement, and this was a special Friday for Central High's student body. The occasion for all the **hoopla** was a big football game that night with Baton Rouge, **their archrival**. People had been lingering about the stairwells, cheering, and waving pom-poms, making those areas particularly hazardous for the nine of us.

The stairwells were huge, open caverns that spiraled upward for several floors, providing ample opportunity to hurl flying objects, dump liquids, or entrap us in dark corners. As I descended the stairwell, **it dawned on me** that except for

....

how you'all will get along if you'll be okay
hoopla excitement
their archrival the team they really wanted to beat
it dawned on me I realized

Danny, I was almost alone. There should have been many more people around because it was a class break.

"Look out, Melba, now!" Danny's voice was so loud that I flinched. "Get down!" he shouted again as what appeared to be **a flaming stick of dynamite** whizzed past and landed on the stair just below me. Danny pushed me aside as he stamped out the flame and grabbed it up. At breakneck speed he dashed down the stairs and handed the stick to another soldier, who sped away. Stunned by what I had seen, I backed into the shadow on the landing, too shocked to move.

"You don't have time to stop. Move out, girl." Danny's voice sounded cold and uncaring. I supposed that's what it meant to be a soldier—to survive.

After gym class, Danny met me in the hall with some unfortunate news. "You're going to your first **pep rally**," he said, concern on his face.

Going to a pep rally was rather like being thrown in with the lions to see how long we could survive. A pep rally meant two thousand students in a huge room with endless opportunity to mistreat us. As I climbed the stairs, I **longed to sprint** to the front door and escape.

"They won't allow me to go in with you," Danny whispered. "But I'll be somewhere outside here."

I didn't respond; I was too preoccupied with finding a safe route into the rally. Nothing had frightened me more than suddenly being **folded** into the flow of that crowd of white

---

a flaming stick of dynamite a type of bomb; an explosive
pep rally school assembly
longed to sprint wanted to run
folded mixed

students as they moved toward the auditorium. Maybe it was because they were all so excited that I got in and to my seat without much hassle. Once settled, I was delighted that Thelma was sitting only a few feet away. Nevertheless, I couldn't relax because I was crammed into that dimly lit room among my enemies, and I knew I had to keep watch every moment. I ignored the activity on stage **in favor of keeping my guard up**.

Over the next twenty minutes, I **worked myself into a frenzy** anticipating what might happen. My stomach was in knots and my shoulder muscles like concrete. I decided I had to **settle myself down**. I repeated the Twenty-Third Psalm. All at once, everybody was standing and singing the school song, "Hail to the Old Gold, Hail to the Black." Some students were snickering and pointing at me as they sang the word "black," but I didn't care. It was over, and I was alive and well and moving out of the auditorium.

Suddenly, I was being shoved backward, toward the corner, very hard. A strong hand knocked my books and papers to the floor as three or four football-player types squeezed me into a dark corner beneath the overhang of the auditorium balcony. One of them **pinned** me against the wall. Someone's forearm pressed hard against my throat, choking me. I couldn't speak. I could hardly breathe.

"We're gonna make your life hell, nigger. You'all are gonna go screaming out of here, taking those nigger-loving soldiers with you."

Just as suddenly as I had been pinned against the wall, I was

....

in favor of keeping my guard up so I could protect myself
worked myself into a frenzy became very nervous
settle myself down relax
pinned trapped

released. I stood still for a moment, holding on to my throat, gasping, trying to catch a good breath. I **stooped** to pick up my things, careful to keep a watch around me. I stumbled back into the flow of the crowd. I couldn't stop coughing, and my throat felt as though I would never speak again. In the distance I saw Danny standing in the hallway, facing the door of the auditorium.

"What's the matter?"

"Some guy tried to choke me," I whispered in a raspy voice.

"And you did nothing?"

"What could I do?" Talking hurt my throat.

"You've gotta learn to defend yourself. You kids should have been given some training in **self-defense**."

"Too late now," I said.

"It's never too late. It takes a warrior to fight a battle and survive. This here is a battle if I've ever seen one."

I thought about what Danny had said as we walked to the principal's office to prepare to leave school. I knew for certain something would have to change if I were going to stay in that school. Either the students would have to change the way they behaved, or I would have to **devise** a better plan to protect myself. My body was **wearing out** real fast.

Later that evening, after Grandma put a warm towel on my throat, I fell into bed, exhausted. In my diary I wrote:

After three full days inside Central, I know that integration is a much bigger word than I thought.

It's harder, more effort than expected

....

stooped bent down

self-defense how to protect yourselves

devise make, develop

wearing out getting tired

138

10

At the end of my first exhausting week at Central High, I decided to **claim Saturday for my very own**. That's why I set my alarm clock for 4 A.M. I wanted a slice of the fresh, still morning all to myself. What I liked most was the absolute silence inside my head and heart—silence I had not enjoyed for so long. Most of all, I wanted to be alone so I could search for the part of my life that existed before integration, the Melba I was struggling to **hold on to**.

I had also promised myself that I wasn't going to turn on the news, read the newspaper, talk, read, or write about integration. I would listen to records, read my *Seventeen* and *Ebony* magazines, and write in my diary. I thought I'd never again be sitting on my bed, nestled between my huge white lace pillows and my stuffed animals, just like a normal girl. I was trying hard not to face the **notion** growing inside me that I was no longer normal, no longer like my other friends.

Later that morning when the family sat down together for breakfast, I couldn't believe that Mama was reading the paper over the breakfast table, something we were forbidden to do.

....

claim Saturday for my very own spend Saturday doing only what I wanted to do

hold on to still be

notion thought, idea

"I see here where the head of the FBI is angry at Faubus for telling lies about the FBI holding those schoolgirls in custody." Mother showed me the *Gazette* headline and the first part of the article.

J. EDGAR HOOVER ANGERED
BY FAUBUS REPORT OF FBI

September 28, 1957: FBI Director J. Edgar Hoover accused Governor Faubus of Arkansas of **disseminating falsehoods** by saying FBI agents held teenagers **incommunicado** for hours of questioning.

"He's really **fired up** the segregationists," Grandma said.

I shut my mind off—I couldn't listen. Their talk made me queasy. When I couldn't stand it any longer I had to speak up. "We're gonna only talk about good things," I said, gulping my last sip of milk. "No Central High talk."

"Deal," Grandma said, standing to clear the table.

By ten we all piled into the car and started off for our big adventure. Grandma had offered to buy me a new store-bought dress—I couldn't believe my ears. Then Mama made her announcement.

"Vince telephoned. He's asked me if you could go with him to church tomorrow, then out **for a bite**. I said yes, provided the two of you come home to have dinner with us."

Saturday night we sat watching *Wagon Train* and *The Sid*

....

disseminating falsehoods telling lies
incommunicado without letting them talk to their families
fired up angered
for a bite to eat

140

Caesar Show on television, and all the while I couldn't stop thinking about Sunday morning with Vince, especially since we were going to his mother's church. At the same time, I wanted to keep Saturday, because it had indeed been my day. Grandma decided we wouldn't answer the phone, so she put it in the cedar chest. Only the shotgun leaning in the corner near her chair reminded me that things were different.

When Sunday actually came around, I was **in a real dither over** my date. I couldn't eat breakfast. Instead, I worked on new hairstyles in front of the mirror. My ponytail was absolutely childish, so I tried **an upsweep, a swatch** over the eye like Gloria Swanson, and a pouf like Elizabeth Taylor. Unfortunately, the ponytail looked best on me.

Not knowing how girls were supposed to behave on dates made me nervous. I kept thinking about what to do or say. I thought about the women in novels I'd read and in the true romance magazines and on the **soaps**. I'd try to behave like them.

When Vince arrived, I headed for the living room. Mother stopped me in the hallway and took both my hands in hers. She held me at arm's length, looking me over as if she were trying to **preserve** that moment in her mind. "Your first real date," she whispered. "I know you are a good girl, and I love you."

Then I was with Vince. He looked down at me, reaching out to hand me a dozen roses, my first roses, just like in the magazines and on *Stella Dallas* on the radio. Red roses.

I whispered my thank-you. I saw the clock on the wall and

....

in a real dither over really excited about
an upsweep, a swatch putting my hair up with some hair
soaps shows on television
preserve keep, remember

with **a sinking heart** realized that in twenty-four hours it would be Monday morning. I would be going back to school, back to Central High.

The date went better than I expected. After a while I relaxed and stopped worrying so much about what to say and do. The minister at Vince's mother's church mentioned my name and had the congregation say a special prayer for me. I could see by the look on Vince's face that he felt proud to be with me. Even dinner with my family went well until Grandma India mentioned news of Central High. The Mothers' League was asking that the 101st be removed from inside the school or at least **cut to a bare minimum**.

Later I lay in bed unable to sleep. The joy from my date with Vince was **overshadowed by** my uncertainty about tomorrow at Central High. I **tossed and turned** all night, worrying that the soldiers would be gone the next day.

When I arrived at school on that Monday morning, I had only one thought—find Danny and the 101st. He was right there, just as he had been in the days before. I kept looking back to see him because I had that nagging feeling he would be leaving all too soon.

That evening I wrote in my diary:

A girl smiled at me today, another gave me directions, still another boy whispered the page I should turn to in our textbook. This is going to work. It will take a lot more patience and more

....

a sinking heart sadness
cut to a bare minimum have fewer soldiers there
overshadowed by almost forgotten because of
tossed and turned could not sleep

strength from me, but it's going to work. It takes more time than I thought. But we're going to have integration in Little Rock.

GUARD TAKES OVER AT SCHOOL
—*Arkansas Democrat*, Tuesday, October 1, 1957

I arrived at school Tuesday morning, fully expecting that I would be greeted by the 101st soldiers and escorted to the top of the stairs. Instead, we were left at the curb to **fend for** ourselves. As we approached the stairs, we were greeted by taunting catcalls and the kind of behavior students had not dared to **exhibit in the face of** the 101st.

"Where are your pretty little soldier boys today?" someone cried out.

"You niggers ready to die just to be in this school?" asked another.

Squeezing our way through the hostile group gathered at the front door, we were blasted by shouts of "Nigger, go home. Go back to where you belong." At every turn, we were faced with more taunts and blows. There were no 101st soldiers at their usual **posts** along the corridors.

And then I saw them. **Slouching** against the wall were members of the Arkansas National Guard, looking on like spectators at a sports event—certainly not like men sent to guard our safety.

I wanted to turn and run away, but I thought about what

···

fend for take care of
exhibit in the face of show in front of
posts places
Slouching Leaning

Danny had said: "Warriors survive." I tried to remember his stance, his attitude, and the courage of the 101st on the battlefield. Comparing my tiny challenge with what he must have faced made me feel more confident. I told myself I could handle whatever the segregationists **had in store for** me. But I **underestimated them**.

Early that morning a boy began to taunt me as though he had been assigned that task. First he greeted me in the hall outside my shorthand class and began pelting me with bottle-cap openers, the kind with the sharp claw at the end. He was also a master at walking on my heels. He hurt me until I wanted to scream for help.

Not long before the end of the school day, I entered a dimly lit rest room. The three girls standing near the door seemed to ignore me. Their passive, silent, almost pleasant greeting made me uncomfortable, and the more I thought about their attitude, the more it concerned me. At least when students were treating me harshly, I knew what to expect.

Once inside the stall, I was even more alarmed at all the movement, the feet shuffling, the voices whispering. It sounded as though more people were entering the room.

"Bombs away!" someone shouted above me. I looked up to see a flaming paper **wad** coming right down on me. Girls were leaning over the top of the stalls on either side of me. Flaming paper floated down and landed on my hair and shoulders. I jumped up, trying to pull myself together and at the same time duck the flames and stamp them out. I brushed the **singeing**

....

had in store for planned to do to

underestimated them did not know how bad they were

wad ball

singeing burning

ashes away from my face as I frantically grabbed for the door to open it.

"Help!" I shouted. "Help!" The door wouldn't open. Someone was holding it—someone strong, perhaps more than one person. I was trapped.

"Did you think we were gonna let niggers use our toilets? We'll burn you alive, girl," a voice shouted through the door. "There won't be enough of you left to worry about."

I felt the kind of panic that stopped me from thinking clearly. My right arm was singed. The flaming wads of paper were coming at me faster and faster. I could feel my chest muscles tightening. I felt as though I would die any moment. The more I yelled for help, the more I inhaled smoke and the more I coughed.

Please, God, help me, I silently **implored**. I had to hurry. I might not be able to **swat** the next one and put it out with my hands. Then what? Would my hair catch fire? I had to stop them. I picked up my books and tossed one upward as hard as I could, in **a blind aim** to hit my attackers.

I heard a big thud, then a voice cry out in pain and several people scuffle about. I tossed another and then another book as fast and as hard as I could. One more of **their number** cursed at me. I had hit my target.

"Let's get out of here," someone shouted as the group hurried out the door. In a flash, I leaped out of the stall, trying to find my things. I decided I wouldn't even bother reporting my problem. I just wanted to go home. I didn't care that I smelled

....

implored prayed, begged
swat hit
a blind aim a desperate try
their number the girls

of smoke or that my blouse was singed. Later when my friends asked what happened, I didn't even bother to explain.

The experiment of doing without the 101st had apparently been a **fiasco**. By the end of the day more than one of us had heard talk that the 101st had been brought back.

Still, despite all our complaints, there were a few students who tried to reach out to us with smiles or offers to sit at our cafeteria tables; some even accompanied us along the halls. Each of us noticed, however, that those instances of friendship were shrinking rather than growing. There was no doubt that the **hard-core troublemakers** were increasing their activities, and without the men of the 101st, they increased a hundredfold.

When we arrived at school on Thursday morning, I noticed right away that there was a different kind of tension, as though everyone was waiting for something awful to happen, only we didn't know what. We had heard rumors of a planned student protest. I could see groups of students standing in the halls instead of in class where they would normally have been.

Just before first period, more students began walking out of classes. Rumors about a big event **reverberated** throughout the school. I could see and feel a new level of restlessness and a deepening sense of hostility. I was on edge, waiting for disaster any moment, like dynamite or a group attack or I didn't know what. "They're hangin' a nigger, just like we're gonna hang you," someone muttered. That's when I learned that some of those who walked out had assembled at the vacant lot at Sixteenth and Park across from the school, where they hanged

....

fiasco failure; bad idea
hard-core troublemakers really mean people
reverberated were talked about

and burned a straw figure.

That demonstration set the tone of the day. **Belligerent** student protests were firing up the already hostile attitude inside the school. Danny broke the rules by coming closer and talking to me—warning that we had to stay alert, no matter what.

Near the end of the day I was walking down a dimly lit hallway, with Danny following, when I spotted a boy coming directly toward me **on a collision course**. I tried to move aside, but he moved with me. I didn't even have time to call for help.

The boy flashed a shiny black object in my face. The sudden pain in my eyes was so intense, so sharp, I thought I'd die. It was like nothing I'd ever felt before. I couldn't hear or see or feel anything except that throbbing, searing fire centered in my eyes. I heard myself cry out as I let go of everything to **clutch at** my face.

Someone grabbed me by my ponytail and pulled me along very fast, so fast I didn't have time to resist. The pain of being dragged along by my hair was almost as intense as that in my eyes. Hands grabbed my wrists and pried my hands from my face, **compelling** me to bend over. Then cold, cold liquid was splashed in my eyes. The water felt so good. My God, thank you! The pain was subsiding.

"Easy, girl, easy. You're gonna be fine." It was Danny's voice, his hands holding my head and dousing my eyes with water.

"I can't see," I whispered. "I can't see."

"Hold on. You will."

Over and over again, the cold water flooded my face. Some

....

Belligerent Violent, Angry
on a collision course trying to run into me
clutch at hold, grab
compelling forcing

of it went into my nose and down the front of my blouse. Bit by bit I could see the sleeve of Danny's uniform, see the water, see the floor beneath us. The awful pain in my eyes had turned into a bearable sting. My eyes felt dry, as though there were **a film drawn** tight over them.

"What was that?"

"I don't know," Danny said, "maybe some kind of alkaline or acid. The few drops that got on your blouse faded the color immediately. Hey, let's get you to the office so we can report this. You gotta get to a doctor."

"No. No," I protested.

"Why not?"

"School's almost over, I wanna go home, right now. Please, please don't make me. . ." I felt tears. I knew he hated me to cry, but the thought of going to the office made me crazy. I couldn't handle having some hostile clerk telling me I was **making mountains out of molehills**.

"Calm down. You can do what you want but—"

"No, home right now," I said, **cutting Danny off**.

A short time later, an optometrist examined my eyes and studied the spots on my blouse. He put some kind of soothing substance into my eyes and covered them with eye patches. As I sat there in the dark, I heard him say. "Whoever kept that water going in her eyes saved the quality of her sight, if not her sight itself. She'll have to wear the patch overnight. She'll have to be medicated for a while. She'll need to wear glasses for **all close work**. I'd really like to see her wear them all the time. I'll need

----

a film drawn something pulled

making mountains out of molehills complaining for no reason

cutting Danny off not letting Danny finish

all close work things like reading and writing

to see her once a week until we're certain she's all right."

Glasses, all the time. I thought. No boy wants to date a girl with glasses.

Despite the doctor's instructions to wear an eye patch for twenty-four hours, I had to take it off. I couldn't let the reporters see me with the patch because they would ask questions and make a big deal of it.

By the time we got home it was seven o'clock, and I wasn't very talkative for the waiting reporters. Once inside I fell into bed, too exhausted to eat dinner. "Thank you, God," I whispered, "thank you for saving my eyes. God bless Danny, always."

BEFORE YOU MOVE ON...

1. **Conclusions** Why didn't Melba want reporters to know about her attacks?

2. **Evidence and Conclusions** Give 2 examples that show that the attacks became more dangerous.

LOOK AHEAD Read pages 150–167 to learn what the nine students said to their attackers.

11

On some days I found myself thinking every waking moment about nothing else but my safety—consumed with learning skills that would keep me alive. When would someone **get the best of me**, and how could I **head them off**? By October 11, I had made myself ill with what appeared to be flu. That Friday, I stayed home from Central and snuggled down into my bed where it was safe.

I was well aware that my illness was more sadness and exhaustion than flu. I knew I had to get myself together because the next day I was supposed to meet with some of the eight others and some hard-core segregationist student leaders for a discussion that might lead to an understanding. To insure my speedy recovery, Grandma **came after me with castor oil**. I protested, but I knew it was no use.

"It's too bad you have to miss a day of school." Mother Lois fluffed my pillows and tightened the sheet at the bottom of my bed. Dressed in her tan gabardine teaching suit with black blouse, she was off to school. "Let's hope you'll be well enough to attend tomorrow."

....

get the best of me really hurt me

head them off stop them

came after me with castor oil made me take bad-tasting medicine

I knew very well I would have to force myself to attend. It would be the first time ever that segregationist student leaders would be coming to talk to us integrating students in a reasonably safe place where we all could **speak our minds**. It was sponsored by a Norwegian reporter, Mrs. Jorumn Rickets, who had set it up with Ernie, Minnijean, and me, and the group **spotlighted as staunch troublemakers**: Sammy Dean Parker, Kaye Bacon, and their crowd. Sammy Dean Parker had been seen in the newspaper embracing Governor Faubus as she thanked him for keeping us out of school.

People referred to the meeting as a possible turning point, a time of coming together. I had thought about nothing else for several days. I even dreamed that we would go to the meeting, and afterward things would calm down considerably at school.

It was that hope that made me drag myself out of bed on Saturday morning and head for the Parish Hall of St. Andrew's Cathedral. Upon arrival I learned the meeting would be recorded by the National Broadcasting Company for future use on a network radio show. I hoped that wouldn't change our being able to speak our minds.

The meeting room was a stark white setting, with mahogany straight-back chairs. It was the kind of place that could well inspire a deep, honest talk that might help us get along with one another. Mrs. Rickets, a woman of medium stature with blond hair pulled to the nape of her neck, began asking questions.

Joseph Fox, **labeled a Central moderate** because he didn't violently oppose our presence, said, "I lay the whole blame for

....

speak our minds say what we really thought

spotlighted as staunch troublemakers thought to be the most likely to cause trouble

labeled a Central moderate known as a person with no strong opinion about segregation this thing in Governor Faubus's lap. We wouldn't have had nearly so much trouble if he hadn't called out the National Guard."

"That's not so. I think our governor is trying to protect all of us," said Sammy Dean Parker. "He said we'd have to integrate, but he has to prepare us."

Ernie said, "All we want is an education and to be able to go to school and back home safely."

When Mrs. Rickets asked why some of the white children objected to going to school with us, Sammy Dean replied: "Well, it's racial, marrying each other."

"School isn't a **marriage bureau**," Ernie said.

"We don't have to **socialize**," I said.

Kaye Bacon said she had heard rumors that we wanted to **"rule" over** them.

"I don't think you know much about our people. I don't think you ever tried to find out," Minnijean said.

Kaye admitted she hadn't tried to understand much about us until that meeting.

"We're scared to death five hundred of you'all are gonna be coming into school," Sammy Dean said.

The white students also expressed their feelings about the troops. Several times they spoke of their outrage at having soldiers in their school. "How do you think we like being escorted in and out of school?" I said. "How do you think we like not knowing who will hit us and when or where we'll be attacked?"

....

marriage bureau place to find a marriage partner
socialize be friends
"rule" over be in charge of

Later in *The New York Times*, Sammy Dean Parker and Kaye Bacon said that as a result of the meeting they now had a new attitude. One headline in the *Gazette* read: "Two Pupils Tell of Change in Attitude on Segregation."

Sammy Dean Parker was quoted as saying, "The Negro students don't want to go to school with us any more than we want to go with them. If you really talk with them, you see **their side of it**. I think the NAACP is paying them to go."

When I read her statement, I realized Sammy hadn't understood at all our reason for attending Central High. I wondered where on earth she thought there was enough money to pay for such brutal days as I was enduring. I wouldn't know how much money to charge for all the good days I wasn't having in my old high school with friends who liked me. What price could anyone set for the joy and laughter and peace of mind I had given up?

By the time I returned to school on Wednesday, things had **deteriorated**. The headlines that day read:

101ST DIVISION CUT BACK FORCE TODAY; ½ GOING BACK TO KENTUCKY

Until that time, when soldiers were taken away it was only to Camp Robinson—**a stone's throw away**. The announcement of their departure to Kentucky gave segregationists reason to celebrate, and **it was evident** in the students who bragged about their renewed hope of getting rid of us.

....

their side of it how they feel about it
deteriorated gotten worse
a stone's throw away which was very close
it was evident you could see the joy

As I stepped into the hallway, just for an instant the thought of fewer troops terrified me. But the warrior growing inside me squared my shoulders and put my mind on alert to do whatever was necessary to survive. I tried hard to remember everything Danny had taught me. I discovered I wasn't frightened in the old way anymore. Instead, I felt my body muscles turn **steely** and my mind strain to focus. I had to take care of myself. I could really depend only on myself for protection.

A new voice in my head spoke to me with military-like discipline: Discover ink sprayed on the contents of your locker—don't fret about it, deal with it. Get another locker assigned, find new books, get going—don't waste time brooding or taking the hurt so deep inside. Kicked in the shin, tripped on the marble floor—assess the damage and do whatever is necessary to remain mobile. Move out! Warriors keep moving. They don't stop to lick their wounds or cry.

By mid-October, there were fewer and fewer 101st guards and fewer Arkansas National Guardsmen. We quickly learned that the presence of the 101st had **lulled** us into a false sense of security. The segregationist students were just **biding their time until they could make their move**. As the guards were reduced in number, our attackers revved up a full campaign against us. The less visible the 101st, the more we suffered physical and verbal abuse.

On Monday, October 28, Mrs. Huckaby notified us in writing that we were to contact our parents to come to a

....

steely strong

lulled tricked

biding their time until they could make their move waiting until the military left so they could do something really bad meeting in School Superintendent Blossom's office, downtown, at 4:45 P.M. That last-minute request meant Mother Lois had to rush over from her teaching job in North Little Rock. But it was necessary, because we all hoped that meeting would signal the beginning of the school officials' willingness to do something about the incredible increase in attacks against us. I couldn't imagine what else they'd want to discuss.

As we climbed the stairs with our parents to the meeting in Superintendent Blossom's office, we all had one thing on our minds—that school officials provide a **concrete** plan to stop the abuse by Central High's hard-core segregationist students.

Thirty minutes into that meeting, neither Blossom nor any of his people had addressed the issue we had told him we were anxious to discuss. Instead, all the school officials present were giving us the same **song and dance** about our not responding to our attackers in order to maintain peace. They were lecturing us on "the proper attitude" and the responsibility of our parents. There were no words from them about how they were going to take any responsibility for keeping students from abusing us.

"Excuse me," Mother Lois said, suddenly rising to her feet, interrupting Superintendent Blossom midsentence. I was frightened to see her standing there so tiny, wringing her hands nervously. "What I want to know is whether or not you have any specific plans for protecting our children."

"That's none of your business," Blossom replied in a rude tone.

"Oh, I'd say it's very much my business." Mother's words

....

concrete real, working
song and dance talk, lecture

came **rapid-fire**. Still he ignored her, continuing his **rhetoric** as before. Silence fell over the room. She interrupted him once more. "As parents we have a right to know how you will protect our children."

Blossom continued his meaningless comments, ignoring her as she stood there for several minutes expecting him to answer her. Finally she took her seat. Her face was red with anger and embarrassment. I felt that by **disrespecting Mother that way**, the superintendent was disrespecting all of us seated in that room. I was very angry with the others, especially the fathers, who did not stand up to defend my mother. The humiliation and fear I felt so upset me that I couldn't consider anything that was said during the remainder of the meeting. Nevertheless, it was clear by the time we left for home that nothing had been resolved. ⸜

On one of the first days of November, Minnijean arrived at my house after school to show me *Life* magazine. It had a full-page picture of my back in it. There I was, ponytail and all, saluting the flag. It wasn't the first time we'd seen ourselves in print or on television, but we giggled at the wonder of it all—Miss Minnijean and Miss Melba could now be seen on the pages of *Life*, *Look*, or *The New York Times*.

As Minnijean and I spent time together that evening, I could tell she was beginning to be deeply affected by what was being done to her at Central High. She seemed especially vulnerable to the **isolation** we were all struggling to cope with.

....

rapid-fire quickly
rhetoric speech, lecture
disrespecting Mother that way treating Mother poorly
isolation loneliness

She had decided she would be accepted by white students if she could just show them how beautifully she sang. She was almost obsessed with finding an opportunity to perform her music on stage. She said she was definitely going to participate in a school program and had in fact already **made inquiries** about it.

Little did we know that even while we were discussing her performing in school programs, the Central High Mothers' League was preparing to make a bigger fuss than ever before to exclude her. But their threats did not stop Minnijean.

I wondered whether or not she had considered that the audience would **boo her off the stage**. Did she figure they would be enraptured by her performance? I shuddered at the thought of what the students would say or do to her if she made it.

When I talked to Ernie about my concerns, he brushed them aside. As usual, he was **taking the situation in stride**. Even when he was punched with punishing blows or was kicked to the floor, he kept a positive attitude. I liked his attitude even when I didn't agree with his view.

Like me, Thelma was very concerned about Minnijean. We talked about how we could convince her to stop pushing to participate. Each of us was hearing increasingly negative responses to her desire to do so. It was clear to us that both students and outsiders would take the opportunity to make a huge issue of her request.

Terry was philosophical about it: Let her try and she'll learn her lesson, once and for all. I could see Terry becoming more

....

made inquiries asked
boo her off the stage hate her; heckle her
taking the situation in stride acting as if nothing was wrong

fatalistic about our predicament. His hopes that we could change people's minds were visibly reduced. He was nervous, not as cheerful, not humming his funny tunes.

Stress was beginning to tell on Gloria, too. She was clamming up, becoming solemn. I could almost see her mind working to try to set things right so she could keep going in her meticulous way.

Elizabeth had never fully regained her composure following her awful encounter with the mob. Continued harassment was also taking its toll of her. She reacted by becoming silent and withdrawn. When I discussed Minnijean's predicament with Elizabeth, she appeared alarmed and agreed that we ought not attract unnecessary attention to ourselves.

Carlotta strained to keep smiling. Although she often **took a lot of heat**, especially in gym class, she tried to make the best of it, as did Jeff. Like the two other boys, Jeff was taking a lot of brutal physical punishment. He was quick on his feet, but he often got trapped in gym class or in corners of the hall, where he was kicked and punched.

Whenever we **compared notes**, we all agreed: the students' attitudes **had become polarized**. We felt it would be best for Minnijean to back off, but none of us could talk her out of it. She was adamant. The more we pleaded, the more determined she seemed to become.

Only during fleeting moments did I allow myself to have fantasies of what it might be like to sing with the chorus or perform in the Thanksgiving program. My hopes of being

....

fatalistic extremely negative

took a lot of heat was attacked

compared notes talked about it

had become polarized could not be changed

a part of normal activities had long since faded. I refused to **set myself up for disappointment**. I simply wanted to make it through the year alive and uninjured. I resigned myself to devoting all my energy to that goal.

I was surprised when I was invited to speak to the students who attended chapel, a fairly safe corner of the school. It had been the one place where I had found brief moments of peace on those days when I arrived early enough to go there. I agonized over the invitation, but finally Grandma made it easy for me. "This is your opportunity to **witness**."

"But what if they throw things?"

"In the house of the Lord? Surely not. These white folks aren't **heathens**. While you speak, they will come to understand you are all worshipping the same Lord." So I prepared my talk, but I kept my invitation to myself. I didn't want to hurt Minnijean's feelings, given the heroic effort she was making to convince school officials to allow her to sing on stage.

It was our tradition each year to sort through our toys and clothing at Thanksgiving and give away all the things we didn't need or use, as well as two things dear to us that we would especially like to keep.

"Conrad, have you got that train boxed yet?"

"Not yet, Grandma."

"When, Conrad?" Mother said as she dried the dinner dishes and handed them to me to put away. She and Grandma had been trying all day to get Conrad to see things their way.

"Melba's giving away her favorite blouse," Grandma said.

....

set myself up for disappointment put myself in a situation that would only disappoint me

witness share your thoughts; share your love of God

heathens people who would disrespect God

"And she's donating her favorite cord skirt and a pair of shoes." She glanced at Conrad to see whether or not her prodding was affecting his **stingy** attitude.

"Melba likes suffering and doing without; that's why she goes to Central. But why do I have to?"

"Where did you get a notion like that about your sister?"

"Clark said that's what his folks say because Sis stays in that white school, being mistreated every day."

"Her staying there means she has made a promise that she intends to keep, because she told God she would and she doesn't want to **let herself and God down**," Mother Lois said, walking over to look Conrad in the eye. "So you must explain that to Clark the next time he inquires about your sister's motives."

"Yes, ma'am. But I'm not giving up the train. It's mine."

"Let's get down to basics, boy. If you don't **ante up**, you won't get any Thanksgiving dinner, and nobody will play Monopoly with you for a full week."

Conrad's eyes got large and his forehead wrinkled as he let go of the train's engine and Grandma placed it in the gift box with our other contributions.

U.S. OFFICIALS DROP PLANS TO **PROSECUTE AGITATORS** AT SCHOOL—WON'T PRESS ACTION AGAINST MOB LEADERS
—*Arkansas Gazette*, Thursday, November 21, 1957

··

stingy bad, selfish
let herself and God down disappoint herself and God
ante up give up the train
PROSECUTE AGITATORS PUNISH PEOPLE CAUSING TROUBLE

Based on **an assurance** by local authorities that they would maintain order, the federal government announced it would **back off** and not even prosecute segregationist mob leaders.

The segregationists' leaders were celebrating their victories, and the students at school were letting us know about their triumph.

And even as our problems with segregationists multiplied yet again, Minnijean focused on her audition for the **glee club** and Christmas show. She had worked herself up into a real dither. Time and time again, Thelma and I had tried to talk her out of participating, but she wouldn't listen. Moments before the tryouts got under way, I stood in the doorway of the auditorium, nervously wringing my hands as Minnijean tried to register.

Mrs. Huckaby wore a pleasant smile as she explained to Minnijean that the day to register for the tryouts had long since passed, and they couldn't violate the rules for her. We knew at once that she had been tricked. Had school officials been sincere about offering Minnijean the opportunity, they would have been clear about the terms for participating. Blinking back tears, Minnijean turned to us, then walked away. Thelma and I trailed behind, trying our best to **console her**. ✐

∾   ∾   ∾

On Monday, November 25, I prepared myself to speak to 250 students gathered for Central High's early morning chapel

....

an assurance a promise; a guarantee
back off not interfere
glee club singing club
console her make her feel better

service. As I walked toward the front of the room and faced those white students, all staring at me, my knees felt weak and the back of my neck was tight. I stood at a podium in a room filled with people who didn't **relish** my speaking to them.

Taking a deep breath, I began the talk I had practiced in front of the mirror and in front of Grandma and Mama. The light from the window at the back of the room was my focus. Mother Lois had said never to look any single member of the audience in the eye when you're speaking. At first, I garbled some of the words, and then, as I remembered Grandma India's advice, I calmed down. She had said, "God's speaking. You're **merely the instrument** he chooses at this time. God is a wonderful speaker, so you have absolutely nothing to be nervous about." I didn't speak about integration or say things about us or them—I just talked about God and how he cares for each of us.

At first I could tell by the students' expressions that they didn't like what I was saying. Some frowned while others **contorted their faces** to show their contempt. Many had perfectly blank looks, but a few listened intently and nodded their heads in agreement. Afterward, two people came up to congratulate me and ask why I had a Northern accent and used such correct English.

"Northern accent, did they really ask you about that?" Mother Lois grinned as I described my speaking. "You tell them your mama's an English teacher, and in this house we speak only **the King's English**."

....

relish like, enjoy
merely the instrument just the voice
contorted their faces looked angry
the King's English correct and proper English

162

We were discussing my day, sitting in our robes at the dining room table, after dinner and baths, playing Monopoly. The house was **festive**, and we were surrounded by the aroma of mincemeat and sweet potato pies cooking in the oven.

"Any flying objects?"

"Actually, some of them were very nice. You were right, Grandma." She didn't look up. She was preoccupied with examining her next move on the board. We were already resigned to the fact that she would **skunk us all** once again.

"Right, how so?" she mumbled, not taking her attention off the game for even one instant.

"Well, for just that moment, I felt we had something in common, our love of the Lord. I think they felt it, too, because some of them smiled and spoke to me."

"Someday they'll have the courage to be nice to you outside that room of worship."

"I don't think so, Grandma, because they would have to take so much criticism from their friends and families."

"This year is different. It won't always be this way." She rolled the dice, bought the last available property, and once again we'd all been **trounced** by our sweet Grandma, the Monopoly champ.

When Mrs. Bates telephoned to say the nine of us would be gathering for an "official" Thanksgiving dinner to be held at her house Tuesday evening before the holiday, she mentioned that there would be a news conference.

....

festive happy, cheerful
skunk us all beat us all at the game
trounced beaten, defeated

I cringed at the thought. Whenever there was special press coverage on us, the abuse we later suffered at Central was **in direct proportion** to the size and quality of the story printed or aired.

When Mother and I arrived at Mrs. Bates's home for the Thanksgiving dinner, I knew even more people than usual were there, because we couldn't find a place to park. When I entered the spacious living room, there was standing room only. I had never seen so many people, most of them reporters, squeezed into that space under hot glaring lights.

At the center of the room, some of the other nine students, dressed in **Sunday best**, were sitting at a table set with the same care Grandma used on holidays: linen and lace and silver and a beautifully prepared **bird**. Mrs. Bates directed me to a seat, and I squeezed past Jeff and Gloria to get to my place.

Even more reporters with more cameras and equipment packed into the room as we tried to give the impression of having a normal meal. Some of the others were reviewing speeches they had prepared. I hadn't prepared anything, because by now the art of giving an interview **was second nature**, or at least that's what I thought. Once the cameras were rolling and the microphones recording, the questions began to fly.

When Mrs. Bates asked, "Do you kids want white meat or dark meat?" I spoke without thinking: "This is an integrated turkey." The annoyed expression on her face matched the one on Mother's, letting me know that maybe I should have prepared a speech. The reporters began snickering as they

....

in direct proportion equal
Sunday best their best clothes; their church clothes
bird turkey
was second nature had become a normal activity

posed a series of questions on turkeys and integration, calling on me by name to answer. My palms began sweating, and my mouth turned dry. I hadn't meant to **put my foot in my mouth**. I didn't want the others to think I was trying to **steal the spotlight**, but once I had spoken out of turn, "integrated turkey" became the theme.

"You'll live to regret that statement, Melba," Mother said as we were driving home. I knew she was agonizing over the consequences of my frivolity. She was right. I would suffer.

There came a day just before Thanksgiving break, when Danny broke the rules again and came close up to talk to me. He wouldn't say whether or not he was leaving for good, but he behaved in a strange way—saying over and over again, "Take care of yourself, you hear me. Don't bend over to pick up any books or walk in dark corners." He winked and smiled as he backed away, giving me a military salute. I stood frozen in my tracks, holding back the tears.

Over and over again, I asked him if he were going away for good, but he wouldn't tell me. "Just **mind your p's and q's**." He turned on his heels. I couldn't admit to myself it was really true. I turned away and ran in the opposite direction, never looking back—never turning to let him see the tears in my eyes.

From that moment on, whenever I thought about Danny and the 101st being gone for good, I pushed the idea out of my mind because I couldn't bear to deal with it. I just had to pretend it wasn't so, even though some part of me kept saying I truly had to **fend for** myself now.

....

put my foot in my mouth say the wrong thing
steal the spotlight get attention
mind your p's and q's watch what you say and do
fend for take care of

~~ ~~ ~~ *O*

My real Thanksgiving at home was a special day of peace and joy. It was wonderful being with all my relatives, and I was able to convince them not to talk about Central High. For just that day, I felt normal, and I hoped that my life could be that way soon. I **came face-to-face with** reality later that evening as I read the *Gazette* headlines: "Last of 225 GI's Leave School; Arkansas National Guard in Charge." *E*

Thanksgiving night I wrote in my diary:

Danny and the others have truly gone. He didn't even say good-bye. I will always remember this man. How could I forget his name? I will never know if he only behaved that kindly because he was a great soldier or a good person or both.

It doesn't matter. He was wonderful. . . .

I want to remember the names of the other nice 101st soldiers as well—Jody, Marty, Mex, and Goggles.

I wish Danny had told me he was leaving forever. Although I don't know how I could have thanked him in words. I might have cried, and he wouldn't have liked that. I never thought I would have tears in my eyes over some white man. I don't think I'll ever see him again. Thank you, Danny.

---

came face-to-face with confronted; dealt with

9 NEGROES BEGIN 12TH WEEK AT CHS WITH NO **INCIDENTS**
—Arkansas Gazette, Tuesday, December 3, 1957

We wondered how the *Gazette* editors had come to that conclusion since they didn't have anyone inside the school. They were like so many of the adults around us, **content to pretend** that all was well as we began classes at Central High on December 2. But we **knew better**. Our day-to-day experience showed us that the situation was worsening.

"Do all niggers eat integrated turkeys?" one boy shouted, putting his foot out to trip me in the hallway on the way to my first class.

"Ooooops," I said as I stepped on his foot, hard. "Oh, excuse me." I grinned. His face reddened. The subject of the turkey was brought up many more times by the end of the day and not in a **friendly fashion**. The only thing that kept me going was counting the days until Christmas vacation.

....

INCIDENTS PROBLEMS, ATTACKS
content to pretend who wanted to think
knew better knew the integration was not going well
friendly fashion nice way

BEFORE YOU MOVE ON...

1. **Comparisons** Compare why students of both races thought African Americans wanted to attend Central.

2. **Cause and Effect** Reread pages 162–163. What caused Melba to think that the attitudes of white students were starting to change?

LOOK AHEAD Read pages 168–185 to find out how Melba celebrated her birthday.

12

Sweet sixteen? How could I be turning sweet sixteen in just a few days and be a student at Central High, I thought as I entered the side door of the school. Looking around, I wanted to **take care** that no one would bang me on my head or trip me up. I had relished so many dreams of how sweet my sixteenth year would be, and now it had arrived, but I was here in this place.

Sixteen had always seemed the magic age that signaled the beginning of freedom, when Mama and Grandma might **let loose their hold** and let me go out with my friends **on pre-dates**. But with the integration, I was nowhere near being free. And in the midst of everything else, I'd almost forgotten my own birthday. I hadn't even begun preparations.

"Hey, nigger. You here again?" A boy's voice pulled me from my thoughts. A strong hand grabbed my wrist and doubled my arm up behind my back, like a policeman arresting a criminal. Frantically I looked for a teacher or guard. There was none.

"Hey, we got us a nigger to play with." He was shouting to his friends. Soon I'd have several of them on me. I struggled

....

Sweet sixteen? Sixteen years old?
take care be careful; watch out
let loose their hold become less strict
on pre-dates and boys as a group

against him, but it was no use. Then I remembered I'd always been told, "If a fellow's got so little manhood he'd hit a woman, it's up to that woman to relieve him of what **few morsels** of his **masculinity** remain." I bent my knee and jammed my foot backward, **up his crotch**.

"Damn you, bitch," he shouted. "You'll be a dead nigger before this day is over."

Grabbing my purse, I raced down the hall, leaving my textbooks behind. I felt the power of having defended myself. I walked up the stairs to homeroom, only to be greeted by the same two boys who had been taunting me every day. I squared my shoulders and glared at them as I whispered, "I will be here tomorrow and the next day and the next."

THE NINE WHO DARED
—New York Post, Thursday, December 5, 1957

Newspapers across the country started carrying a series of articles and profiles on the nine of us. Central High segregationists used the details to taunt us. The articles gave specific information on what our homes were like, our backgrounds, our hobbies, our **aspirations**—all there was to know about us. Students didn't let up for one minute, chirping on about my folks, my mother's teaching, and things I considered personal and sacred.

When the nine of us compared notes, we discovered we were all facing an increasing barrage of injurious activities.

....

few morsels little bit
masculinity manhood, pride
up his crotch between his legs
aspirations goals, dreams

What was noticeably different was the frequency and the organized pattern of harassment. Teams of students appeared to be assigned specific kinds of torture. One team concentrated on slamming us into lockers, while another focused on tripping us up or shoving us down staircases; still another concentrated on attacks with weapons. Another group must have been told to practice **insidious** harassment inside the classrooms. Still others worked at entrapment, luring the boys into dark corners or the girls into tight spots in isolated passageways. Some continued to use the showers as a means of abuse.

At the same time I was feeling alarmed about rumors of segregationist training programs to sharpen the skills of hooligans inside school. I was also increasingly worried about Minnijean. She was **waging** yet another battle with school officials to get permission to appear with the choral group in the Christmas program. No matter how much Thelma and I tried to convince her to let go of the idea, she wouldn't give up the notion that if she could perform, somehow the white students would see she was talented and therefore accept her.

I **fretted** about Minnijean as I plunged into my birthday party plans, but the more I tried to console her, the less she listened. She was the only one of my eight Central friends I had invited to my party, because I wanted to escape all thoughts of being an integration person. I made her promise not to talk about Central in front of our **Horace Mann** friends.

Not inviting the others made me feel guilty; but had the eight come, I knew I would have been separate—one of the

....

insidious mean but not obvious
waging starting, fighting
fretted worried
Horace Mann other high school

Little Rock Nine and not just plain Melba, a member of my old group. I counted on reconnecting to my friends from my former school. I wanted them to accept me, to take me back into their **fold**. I had personally called or left messages with the parents of all the people on my guest list.

On the morning of my birthday, Saturday, I felt relieved when Minnijean called to say she couldn't come after all because she had a family event that day. Maybe with only me there, I could fade into the group and just this once be one of them.

Vince was the first to arrive, looking a little **ill at ease**. "Good evening, birthday girl," he said, handing me a small box with a bow. I hadn't seen him in a while. I'd almost forgotten how light-skinned he was. With his dark shiny hair piled high and his sideburns, he resembled those sideburners at Central.

"Thanks, I'm glad you came," I said. My mind worked hard to separate the way he looked from the images of the boys who treated me so badly at Central. Vince is one of my people, no matter how white he looks, I told myself. I tried to think about the first date we had and to focus on how much I had liked being with him.

"**Long time no see**," Vince said as I led him into the living room. "You never return my calls."

He was right. Somehow the whole integration thing had even dulled my desire for daydreams about him. He had become **lost in the shuffle**, an afterthought, but I couldn't tell him that. "I think about you," I told him, "especially when Grandma goes to the wrestling matches. I wanted to call." He nodded his head,

....

fold group
ill at ease nervous
Long time no see I have not seen you in a long time
lost in the shuffle less important than integration

but he didn't look like he believed me.

As we continued polite but **strained** talk I kept my eyes on the clock. I unwrapped his gift, squealing with delight at the tiny gold hoop earrings. Mama and Grandma made several trips to bring food in, then take it out for warming, then bring it back. After an hour, when no other guests had arrived, Conrad insisted we begin eating.

The explanation came when my old friend Marsha phoned to say she wouldn't be coming, but she'd **drop off** my birthday present the next day. I had counted on Marsha's coming, she was kind of the leader of the group. If she didn't come, I worried that nobody else would either. Then she **confirmed my worst fears**. She explained that another friend, Ann, was giving her annual Christmas party, and most of the people I invited would be going there. But I knew that Ann's party wouldn't begin before eight. When I asked why they couldn't stop by beforehand, there was a long silence, and then she said, "Melba, the truth is we're all afraid to come to your house."

"Why didn't you say so earlier, when I called?"

"I didn't wanna hurt your feelings. You gotta get used to the fact that you'all are just not one of us anymore. **You stuck your necks out**, but we're not willing to die with you." $\mathcal{E}$

"Marsha, I thought you were my friend." I heard my voice get loud as anger rose in me. "At least you could have told me there was another party going on," I shouted into the receiver, slamming it down.

My feelings were doubly hurt. No one bothered to tell me to

....

strained uncomfortable
drop off bring
confirmed my worst fears said that no one would be coming
You stuck your necks out You took a risk

move my party to another date, and worse yet, they were having the biggest Christmas party of the season without inviting me.

Even though I felt so embarrassed I could die, I kept smiling, trying to pretend to Vince that I wasn't **brokenhearted** about the empty room we sat in with all those balloons on the ceiling and all that food getting cold on the dining room table.

"Let's turn on the TV now, since nobody's coming. That just means more food for us." Conrad's voice sounded like he was speaking through a booming microphone as he burst into the room. **I felt myself cringe** as I watched Vince's face turn red.

"Shush your mouth, boy, and get back into that kitchen." Grandma was trying her best not to look disappointed. But I could see she felt sad for me. I moved toward the dining room and started taking things to the kitchen. **I caught Grandma unaware.** I could see there was moisture in her eyes.

"Don't worry about the party, Grandma. It doesn't matter," I said, touching her shoulder.

"You just sit yourself down and entertain that young man."

"He doesn't want to be entertained. He wants to go to Ann's Christmas party, where everybody is. He's asked me to go with him." I was hoping that since it was my birthday they would make an exception and allow me to go with Vince.

"How can we allow you to go out that way, in public? Don't you see those two white devils parked in their car across the street? They're watching us like always. **Mutt and Jeff** are just waiting for us to make a mistake so's they can hang you. We couldn't rest easy with you out at night that way."

....

brokenhearted upset, angry
felt myself cringe was embarrassed
I caught Grandma unaware. I surprised Grandma.
Mutt and Jeff White segregationists

"Even on my birthday?"

"Especially on your birthday. This day reminds us of how important you are to us. Now, you invite Vince to sit a while. We'll have a nice evening playing games and all."

But Vince clearly wanted to move on to Ann's party. He had promised he would go, and he wanted to be with our friends— only they weren't our friends anymore. They were his. I saw him to the door and stood in the doorway looking at Mutt and Jeff's car parked beneath the streetlight. Grandma was right. It wasn't safe. The integration had **stolen** my sixteenth birthday.

Later that night before I sobbed into my pillow, I wrote:

> *Please, God let me learn how to stop being a warrior. Sometimes I just need to be a girl.*

STEP UP IN RUMORS, INCIDENTS, COMPLAINTS NOTED AT SCHOOL
—*Arkansas Gazette*, Saturday, December 14, 1957

ARMY TO CUT GUARD FORCE AT CENTRAL HIGH SCHOOL BY 432 MEN
—*Arkansas Gazette*, Saturday, December 14, 1957

With four days to go before the Christmas holidays, we were very aware of a **last-minute drive** to get us out of school

....

stolen ruined
STEP UP INCREASE
last-minute drive desperate attempt

174

before the new year. Flyers and cards appeared saying "Two, four, six, eight, we ain't gonna integrate—no, not in '58." There was lots of talk about how we wouldn't come back when the new semester started.

We were all suffering from **extreme fatigue** as we marked our calendars and counted down the moments before the blissful two weeks of Christmas vacation. Most of all I looked forward to feeling safe, to having fun with maybe a party or two, and to lots of lounging in front of the television—that was my plan.

Grandma had already begun shopping, hiding gifts, and testing the Christmas lights so she could replace burnt-out bulbs. She had also begun making dough for Christmas cookies and placing it in the freezer. Mother Lois was eyeballing trees so we'd choose the perfectly shaped one.

On Tuesday, December 17, when we had one more day to go before vacation, five of us entered the cafeteria. Lunchtime was always a hazard, and recently even more so. I had been avoiding the cafeteria, eating my sandwich alone in any safe place I could find. The cafeteria was such a huge place, with so many of our attackers gathered at one time. There were no official-looking adults or uniformed Arkansas National Guardsmen inside. **Without fail**, we knew we could expect some form of harassment.

As always on Tuesday the hot lunch was chili, which Minnijean loved. So while I took my seat with the others, she got in line to buy her chili. Ernie emerged from the line ahead

....

extreme fatigue being very tired; exhaustion
Without fail Every day

of her and sat down at our table. As Minnijean made her way back toward us, her tray loaded down with a big bowl of chili, we saw her hesitate. She had to **inch her way** through a tight spot where mostly boys sat at tables on either side of her path. She had stopped **dead in her tracks**. We all froze, realizing she must be in real trouble. We could see two boys near her—one directly in her path. Something awful was happening, but there was no way any of us could do anything to rescue her. We had been instructed that in such instances we were never to move toward the person in danger for fear of starting a riot.

I was panic-stricken. Minnijean was being hassled by those boys. Snickering among themselves and taunting her, they had pushed a chair directly in front of her. For a long moment, she stood there patiently, holding her tray high above their heads.

It was all I could do to hold on to my chair and not go to help her. Like a broken record, the words played over and over in my head—**intervening on her behalf would blur the lines between** who was the victim and who was the person at fault. If other white students joined the melee to rescue the other side, we'd have a brawl. They outnumbered us at least two hundred to one. Still, I wanted to go to her, move the chair, take her tray, tell her to back up and go another way, do something, anything.

As more and more people realized something was brewing, the chatter in the cafeteria quieted down. I could tell Minnijean was trapped and desperate, and very fast running out of patience. She was talking back to the boys in a loud voice, and there was jostling all around her.

....

inch her way walk very slowly

dead in her tracks completely

intervening on her behalf would blur the lines between
going to help her would confuse people about

Frantically I looked around to see if there were any adults nearby who could be trusted to help. We had come to believe that the vice-principal for girls, Mrs. Huckaby, made some efforts to be fair during these situations, but she was nowhere in sight. I beckoned to Minnijean to go around her hasslers, but she was standing perfectly still. It was as though she were in a trance, fighting within herself.

Later she would explain that the boys had been taunting her, sticking their feet in the aisle to trip her, kicking her, and calling her names. But we were not close enough to see details of the dilemma she faced. All we saw was her wavering as though she were trying to balance herself—and then her tray went flying, spilling chili all over two of the boys.

Everyone was stunned, silent for a long moment. Her attackers sat with astonished looks on their faces as greasy chili dripped down over their heads. All at once, our people who were serving food behind the counter began to applaud. This was greeted by **an ominous** silence, and then loud voices, all chattering at once, as the chili-covered boys stood up. I wondered whether we'd ever get out of there alive. Suddenly a school official showed up, and Minnijean was **whisked** away, while we were hustled out of the cafeteria.

Word got around school immediately. Clusters of people gathered along the hallway, chanting, "Two, four, six, eight, we ain't gonna integrate." Some were applauding and laughing. I wondered why some students were **jubilant**, almost celebrating. I especially noticed that some of the segregationist leaders

....

an ominous a threatening
whisked taken
Word got The story spread
jubilant happy, thrilled

seemed very pleased with themselves.

As I went to my afternoon classes, I couldn't help being very anxious about what was happening to Minnijean that caused such a jovial uproar.

"Looking for your little nigger friend?" one of the students said as I walked down the stairs to study hall. "**She's done got herself suspended**. She can only get back in if the superintendent lets her, and you know what that means." E

"One nigger down and eight to go" was the cry we heard as we left Central High for Christmas vacation. I could hear those declarations shouted even above the festive Christmas carols being played: "One nigger down and eight to go."

....

She's done got herself suspended. She was forced to leave school.

13

NEGRO GIRL IS SUSPENDED FROM SCHOOL
AFTER INCIDENT
—*Arkansas Gazette*, Wednesday, December 18, 1957

My hopes for a blissful two-week respite from Central High over Christmas vacation had been **dashed** by the dilemma we all faced because of Minnijean's suspension. By dumping the chili over the white boys' heads, whether accidentally or not, she had **opened a door through which segregationist leaders announced they would eject all of us**. It was the beginning of the end of Little Rock school integration, they said. Immediately, cards and flyers appeared all over town reading: "One nigger down, eight to go."

Her suspension notice stated that Minnijean could not begin the process to apply for readmission until six school days had passed. Classes would resume on January 3 of the new year.

So instead of the peaceful, happy, safe Christmas vacation I had dreamed of for months, I was **embroiled** in integration meetings and worry. It was that nagging kind of problem that

....

dashed ruined

opened a door through which segregationist leaders announced they would eject all of us given the segregationist leaders an idea to get rid of all of us

embroiled involved

stays at the back of your mind, no matter what else is going on. Will they or won't they let Minnijean back in school, and if they don't, what will it mean to the rest of us?

As I entered the living room early one evening, Grandma was setting up the **manger scene**, gingerly placing each of the crudely carved wooden figures that had been **handed down from** her mother. She wouldn't allow any of us to help for fear we'd drop a piece. What with all her baking and decorating and gift making, this was her favorite time of the year, next to spring planting.

I took a deep breath and sank into the couch, waiting for Mother Lois to get dressed for a party we were to attend to honor the Little Rock Nine.

"Where are you going?" Conrad asked.

"Mama and I are going to a grown-up Christmas party," I answered. I didn't want to make too much of it because I figured he was beginning to feel left out, what with all the fuss being made over me in newspapers and magazines and now a party planned in our honor. The National Organization of Delta Sigma Theta, a professional women's **sorority**, had decided to give us a Christmas party at the Dunbar Community Center. It was the first time some of my own people were saying a public thanks to us. It lightened some of the pain I felt for all those who were critical of our going to Central.

As I entered the community center, sorority women, showing off their high fashion and high spirits, greeted us

....

manger scene Christmas decorations
handed down from given to her by
sorority university club

as though we were very important. They had **made us their secret project**, with members of the nationwide organization mailing gifts and loving notes from across the country to be presented to us that evening.

I was bursting with pride as people said nice things about my courage and about what we nine were doing for **future generations** who would be able to attend integrated schools. It wasn't the kind of party where you have teenage fun, but it was wonderful just the same, especially because I had so few opportunities to socialize.

Minnijean's suspension was mentioned only **in passing**. Despite that worry, we nine enjoyed one another as friends, once outside the pressure we shared at Central High. We compared our gifts, of course. My favorite was a carved mahogany jewelry box. I'll keep this forever and give it to my grandchildren, I thought to myself as I carefully placed it on the nightstand beside my bed later that evening. In my diary I wrote:

> *Tonight I feel love from my own people. Everybody tried to make us happy. There is the tiniest flicker of hope and joy inside me. Maybe things will work out. Please, God, won't you allow Minnijean to come back to school just this once. I promise I'll help her be stronger.*

Christmas Eve was delightful as we sat sipping hot chocolate and wrapping gifts to place under the tree. Each of us traded a

---

made us their secret project been very supportive of us
future generations African American children in the future
in passing briefly

personal gift. If during the year one of us **coveted** something that belonged to another, we might get the temporary loan of that item for January of the new year. We especially looked forward to those gift notes in our stockings. For example, I was thinking about granting Conrad the **privilege of using** my stereo twice a day for one month, but I wasn't certain I could be that generous so I wrote "maybe" on my note to him.

Vince called to say he would come by on Christmas, with Mother's permission. The thought of our being together near the tree on that special day, listening to carols, really **sparked** romantic daydreams. But as always my daydreams were so much better than the reality of being with him because we now had very little in common. He still spent most of our time together questioning me about Central and teasing me about being a celebrity.

Later that evening Papa Will came by to bring his presents. I hadn't seen much of my father since the integration began, but this time he was in a good mood. He didn't bother to say "I told you so," even though his awful predictions about integration causing trouble had for the most part come true. He was pleasant and genuinely concerned. The best part was the surprise he had hidden on the front porch, a brand-new television set with a big screen. He had chosen a special small gift for each of us. The fact that he put lots of time and thought into the gift selection made me feel that despite the way he had behaved, maybe he really did love me.

He and Mama looked at each other **fondly** for just an instant,

....

coveted wanted
privilege of using right to use
sparked started
fondly in a loving way

and it felt as though we were a family again. I sometimes prayed they would get back together. At first Conrad and I had **hoped against hope**. As the years passed, we watched them grow apart in odd ways that made us sad. Rumors around church were that Papa even had a girlfriend now. But just for an instant, Conrad and I eyed each other, both thinking how nice it would be if he stayed. Maybe they would go with us to the family dinner and announce they were getting back together. But then Papa looked at his watch, cleared his throat, and off he went.

> *Dear Diary,*
>
> *It's Christmas Eve and Papa's not coming home to stay. For nine Christmases now I've prayed he would be with us. Maybe it's not gonna happen. Could I please have a nice, new stepfather. Thy will be done. By next Christmas either I want things to be a lot better at Central or I want to be somewhere else, please God. Merry Christmas.*

Christmas dinner with the family was the biggest occasion of the year, a time when we spent the day **catching up on family love and bloodline gossip**, as Grandma called it. We were twenty-seven laughing, chatting people. I had waited all year to see all the relatives who weren't at Thanksgiving.

Even though all of them had definite opinions about my adventures at Central High, I had **vowed** not to talk about it. No matter what it took, I wanted to pretend life was normal again. I wanted the feeling of Christmas before integration.

....

hoped against hope believed they might remarry
catching up on family love and bloodline gossip loving each
other and telling stories about our lives and our families
vowed decided

By late evening, as we sat in front of the fire, singing Christmas carols, I realized maybe I had my wish. I hadn't felt that content since the summer before in Cincinnati.

LITTLE ROCK STORY SECOND ON AP'S BEST LIST
—Arkansas Gazette, Sunday, December 29, 1957

The stories ranged from number one, the launching of **Sputnik**, to President Eisenhower's **stroke** and the passage of the **Civil Rights bill**.

How strange, I thought, to be involved in something that the whole nation considers among its ten most important stories. If it's that important, you'd think somebody would be able to do something to make the Central High students behave themselves. Is it that nobody cares, or nobody knows what to do?

By New Year's Eve, I only thought about Central High perhaps every other hour. Vince had invited me to a party, but of course Grandma and Mama said no. Besides, our famous shadows, Mutt and Jeff, were parked across the street, faithful as hound dogs **in their vigilance**. Although we discussed reporting them to the police, we knew full well that might bring on more trouble. So we simply lived with their being there, watching us. Mother didn't like my coming and going at night even when the party was in my neighborhood. Only on

....

Sputnik a satellite into space
stroke medical problems; illness
Civil Rights bill law giving African Americans more rights
in their vigilance as they watched us every day

rare occasions did any of us go out after dark. Once **dusk** came, we locked all the doors and windows and closed the curtains.

So on New Year's Eve, I sat home completing my list of New Year's **resolutions**.

1. To do my best to stay alive until May 29.
2. To pray daily for the strength not to fight back.
3. To keep faith and understand more of how **Gandhi** behaved when his life was really hard.
4. To behave in a way that pleases Mother and Grandma.
5. To maintain the best attitude I can at school.
6. To help Grandma India with her work.
7. To help Minnijean remain in school—to be a better friend to her.

---

dusk evening

resolutions goals

Gandhi a man who believed in nonviolent protest

BEFORE YOU MOVE ON...

1. **Summarize** How did Melba's friends treat her on her sixteenth birthday? Why?

2. **Irony** Reread page 184. Why was Little Rock as a top story in December, 1957, ironic to Melba?

LOOK AHEAD Read pages 186–203 to find out how the attacks affected Melba.

14

The first school days of the New Year were frightening because without Minnijean we realized any one or all of us could be next. Posters and cards reading "One nigger down and eight to go" were everywhere. Segregationists left no doubt that they were **seizing** Minnijean's suspension as an opportunity to fire up their campaign.

Once we got back into our daily routine, it was evident that segregationists must have spent their holidays thinking up ways to make us miserable. I could feel their electrifying hope of victory all around me: they walked differently, talked differently, and didn't hesitate to shower us with angry words and deeds, letting us know we **were short-timers**.

I had by then **withdrawn from** French class because I wasn't able to concentrate with the combined pressure of the extremely hostile students and coping with everything else. I was also concerned that I couldn't do my best in my English, shorthand, and typing classes, all of which would have been **a breeze** under any other circumstances.

Even before lunch on our first day back, we had all begun

....

seizing using
were short-timers would not be at Central for long
withdrawn from dropped out of
a breeze very easy

to experience a hell we could not have imagined. The rumor was that the White Citizens Council would pay reward money to the person who could **incite** us to misbehave and get ourselves expelled. It was apparent that many students were going for that reward.

On Monday, January 6, Minnijean and her parents met with Superintendent Blossom. She was allowed to return to school Monday, January 13, with the **proviso** that she not respond to her attackers in any way.

A short time after Minnijean's return, a boy doused her with what appeared to be a bucket of soup. She froze in her tracks and did not respond, even as the greasy liquid trickled down her chest and horror painted her face. Afterward a group of perhaps fifty students gathered outside the principal's office to shout cheers for the douser, saying he had **paid her back**. He was suspended, but we were frightened that he had set in motion an all-out soup war that could lead to the drenching of each one of us and guarantee a real brawl if we tried to fight back.

The segregationists were becoming even more vocal, urging the students to harass us at every opportunity. The Central High Mothers' League announced a nighttime rally with the Reverend Westley Pruden, president of the Citizens Council, speaking on "What Race Mixers Are Planning for Us." They issued a special invitation to Central High students. We heard that almost two hundred hard-core segregationist students protested our presence by being absent from school on the day of that rally.

....

incite get, encourage
proviso condition, understanding
paid her back taken revenge

The segregationists organized a **systematic process** for phoning our homes at all hours of the night to harass us. They also phoned our parents at their places of work and any other relatives or friends they could annoy. One day, Terrence's mother rushed into the principal's office, having been called and told her son was seriously injured, only to find the call had been a **hoax**. Repeated bomb threats were telephoned to our homes.

We had real evidence that school officials weren't certain of their ability to protect us, when, on the day of a pep rally, Mrs. Huckaby suggested that Thelma, Minnijean, Elizabeth, and I sit in her office rather than be exposed to the hostility and physical abuse that certainly awaited us.

We were having more frequent meetings with Mrs. Bates and other NAACP officials about our problems. Despite our conversations and all the public declarations that school officials could protect us, the truth was, things were getting worse by the moment.

As determined as everyone else was to have me remain at Central, with each passing day I began to doubt that I was strong enough to **tough it out**. Even as I watched the others weaken, I could feel myself growing weary and nervous. When I had a long period of time alone on a Saturday, I leafed through the pages of my diary. I had not been fully aware of how deeply the turmoil at school was affecting me. I was stunned to see what I had written.

"I wish I were dead." That was **the entry** for several days running, in late January. "God, please let me be dead until the

---

systematic process careful plan

hoax trick, joke

tough it out make it to the end of the year

the entry what I had written

end of the year." I was willing to bargain and plead with God. I revised my request; I just wanted to become invisible for a month or two. I clutched the diary to my chest and wept for a long time. "No," I whispered aloud, "I do wish I were dead." Then all the pain and hurt would be over. I fell to my knees and prayed about it. That's when I knew I should go and talk to Grandma India. I told her about my wish to be dead.

"Good idea," she said. She didn't even look up at me as though she were alarmed after I **whimpered out** my **confession**. Instead, she continued dusting the dining room table. My feelings were hurt. And then she looked me in the eye and said it again. "Good idea! How did you plan going about it?"

"Ma'am?" I wasn't certain I'd heard her. "I said I wish I were dead—did you hear me?"

"And I said, good idea." Her voice was louder as she peered at me with a mischievous expression. "The sooner you get started, the sooner you'll make the segregationists real happy. They'll love broadcasting the headlines across the world." She braced the palm of one hand on the table to balance herself as she paused for a long moment to think. "I've got it. The headlines will read, 'Little Rock heroine gives in to segregationists—kills herself.' "

"What do you mean?" I gasped. I felt really angry that she talked as though she didn't care. She kept on creating new headlines about my death.

"Or maybe they could write: 'Melba Pattillo died by **her own hand** because she was afraid of facing God's assignment for her.' "

....

whimpered out cried and told her
confession wish to be dead
her own hand suicide; killing herself

"Oh, no, ma'am." I slumped down into a chair.

She wouldn't **let up**. "Then, of course, there would be the celebration all the segregationists would plan. Let's see now, I'll bet they would rent the Robinson Auditorium for their party. It would be kinda like the wrestling matches, you know, loud, with all the cheering, singing, and dancing." She looked back down at the scratches on the table and continued dusting. "So do **as you please**, but I'd also think about that moment at which you'd have to face the Lord and explain your decision to him." She ignored me, humming her hymn, "I'm on the Battlefield for My Lord." I stood there for a moment watching her.

That did it. I realized dying wasn't a good idea. I was almost certain God wouldn't allow people to die for only a short while and come back. After that, Grandma arranged for a daily time when I had to come to her room, get down on my knees, and pray with her. Then she and I would talk about what was troubling me and what I would like. We would play Yahtzee or read pages from some fun novel I would choose. Sometimes we'd read through the newspaper together, but only the good things like the launching of an American satellite into orbit that circled the earth in 116 minutes.

During those days I felt so close to her, and I knew I had been silly for wanting to give up. Several times she looked at me and said, "Don't you know, child, how much I love you, how much your mama loves you? Whenever you think about going away from this earth, think about how you'd **break my heart and your brother's heart**. You might as well take your mother

....

let up stop talking about it

as you please what you want

break my heart and your brother's heart make me and your brother very sad with you because she'd **be beside herself**."

She made me get a project I really liked and encouraged me to keep on top of it. I chose the blast-off of the Explorer, the satellite that put our country into the **space race**. I had always been interested in rockets and space. Once I had run away to the Strategic Air Command Base in a nearby town to see if they would allow me to become a pilot. Grandma studied up on the topic, and we talked for hours while she taught me how to do the quilting for Mother's birthday present.

Meanwhile, Mother Lois urged me to give Vince a standing invitation to Sunday supper. I couldn't understand why she was being so nice. I think Grandma talked to her about our conversation, and she was trying to cheer me up. Sometimes Vince came even when I didn't want him to. There were times when I just wanted to stay in my room and think, because I had no energy or desire to do anything else. Everything in me was devoted to being a full-time warrior. When I wasn't actually on the battlefield, surviving, I was thinking about how to do it or worried that I wouldn't be able to make it.

Every day Grandma and I prayed hard for Minnijean to have strength and peace of mind and for all of us to be able to feel God's love for us, even in the face of those who spewed so much hatred our way.

For the second time, on Thursday, February 6, Minnijean was attacked by the boy who dumped soup on her. During the **ruckus** that followed, there was a great deal of confusion. The identity of who attacked and who fought back was not clear.

....

be beside herself not want to live without you
space race competition for space exploration
ruckus disturbance, commotion

Her attackers accused her of **retaliation**. "White trash" were the words they reported her to have said. In addition, they accused her of throwing a purse at a girl.

When she was sent home without receiving a suspension notice, I breathed a sigh of relief. But at the end of the day, Mrs. Huckaby gave Carlotta a sealed envelope to be delivered to Minnijean.

"THEY BOTHER YOU ALL THE TIME," **OUSTED** NEGRO STUDENT CONTENDS
—*Arkansas Democrat*, Thursday, February 13, 1958

In the article that followed, Minnijean explained the pressure she had been under at school. She said she had only had half a white friend at Central, a two-faced girl who **ran hot and cold**. Of the other students she said: "They throw rocks, they spill ink on your clothes, and they call you 'nigger'—they bother you every minute."

I cried for an hour when word came that the envelope sent to Minnijean was a suspension notice. I was devastated when Superintendent Blossom said he would recommend her **expulsion**. But when the NAACP and her parents announced they would push to have a hearing, I kept a glimmer of hope.

I read in the paper that Thurgood Marshall said he didn't know how much more unpleasant treatment we could take at Central High. That night I wrote in my diary:

....

retaliation trying to get revenge
OUSTED SUSPENDED
ran hot and cold was only nice sometimes
expulsion permanent removal from school

I sometimes wish I could change myself into a psychiatrist to determine what makes me such a hated member of this school. Can they really be treating me this way simply because I am brown, that's all.

"Ooooooo, no, no," I heard myself shout as I was walking up the Fourteenth Street stairwell one morning. It wasn't yet 8:40, and I was already the victim of a dousing with raw eggs from someone standing on the stairs above my head. The odor bothered me, but even more, it was the feel of that slimy substance oozing very slowly through my hair and onto my face, while at the same time raw egg slithered over the sweater Aunt Mae Dell had given me for Christmas.

"The nigger's come to have breakfast. I can tell, she's wearing eggs," one boy called. I never said a word back to the group hovering with their ugly catcalls. I knew they were just hoping I'd do or say something that would result in my expulsion. I backed down the stairs and out the door to go home.

"Well, this egg is wonderful for putting moisture in the hair," Grandma said. "Some people use it for that, you know. Maybe we ought to start it on a regular basis." She was trying to wipe out as much as she could; then I would have to bathe and wash my hair. "Hold still," she continued. "After a nice long bath, you can hurry back to school, and this will have been just a **refreshing** break in your morning."

"I've never been so embarrassed."

....

refreshing nice

193

"Oh, I'll bet there've been other times and there'll be more. Embarrassment **is not a life-threatening problem**. It can be washed away with a prayer and a smile, just like this egg is washed away with a little water."

"I know, but it's the same way I feel when they spit on me. I feel like they've taken away my dignity."

"Dignity is a state of mind, just like freedom. These are both precious gifts from God that no one can take away unless you allow them to." As Grandma spoke, she motioned me to turn my head to the other side.

"You could take charge of these mind games, you know."

"How do you mean?"

"Take, for example, this egg in your hair. Suppose you'd have told the boys who did this, 'Thank you,' with a smile. Then you've changed the rules of the game. What they want is for you to be unhappy. That's how they get pleasure."

"Yeah, but that would be letting them win."

"Not exactly. Maybe it would **defeat their purpose**. They win when you respond the way they expect you to. Change the rules of the game, girl, and they might not like it so much."

"They'd think I was crazy."

"They'd think you were no longer their victim."

For the rest of the morning as I walked the halls, amid my hecklers, I couldn't stop thinking about what it would be like to feel as though I were in charge of myself. I always believed Grandma India had the right answer, so I decided to take her advice.

....

is not a life-threatening problem will not kill you

"You could take charge of these mind games, you know." "You can win these fights."

defeat their purpose stop their attacks

As I tried to open a classroom door, two boys pushed it closed. At first I tried to pull it open, but then I remembered changing the rules of the game. I stood up straight, smiled politely, and said in a friendly voice, "Thank you. I've been needing exercise. You've done wonders for my arm muscles." I chatted on and on as if they were my friends. They looked at me as though I were totally **nuts**, then they let go of the door. I felt great power surging up my spine like electricity. I left them standing there looking at each other.

On February 14, Valentine's Day, it snowed. That afternoon, as we stood in the snow waiting for our ride, we were attacked with snowballs filled with rocks. Mr. Eckford, Elizabeth's father, bolted from the car to rescue us, but he, too, was bombarded. Little Rock's finest police officers and members of the federalized National Guard stood by, watching with their arms folded as we were hit time after time. Even when we pleaded for their **assistance**, they did nothing.

When I arrived home, Grandma handed me a large oddly shaped envelope. "I suspect it's a special greeting from that young man you ignore most of the time. After all, it is a special day."

I took the envelope to my room to open it. It was a card from Vince. As I read the beautiful words, I was sad that I couldn't talk to him on the phone or see more of him, but **for the life of me I couldn't** fit him into my schedule. Even my daydreams about him were beginning to fade because integration was

....

nuts crazy

assistance help

for the life of me I couldn't there was no way I could

taking up all the space in my mind.

THREE CHS PUPILS SUSPENDED;
MINNIJEAN BROWN EXPELLED
—*Arkansas Gazette*, Tuesday, February 18, 1958

Minnijean was expelled after a forty-minute hearing. The official announcement of her expulsion was a devastating defeat for us. The fact that the school board at the same time suspended three white pupils, two for wearing "One down, eight to go" cards and one for pushing Gloria down a flight of stairs, didn't **lessen the blow**. The NAACP had counted on getting Minnijean's expulsion reversed, but Blossom and the school board were **adamant in sticking to their conclusion**, despite all the pressure on them.

National NAACP officials arranged for Minnijean to **have a scholarship to** a famous private New York high school called New Lincoln. She would live with the family of a renowned psychologist, Dr. Kenneth Clark. I had read that it was his research that had supported Thurgood Marshall and the NAACP's legal suit that resulted in the 1954 Supreme Court decision to integrate the schools.

It was a fabulous opportunity for her, but all I could think about was how far New York was from Little Rock. We would no longer be able to get together to have our usual talks. At the same time, I tried not to be jealous that Minnijean would be escaping the hell that was my daily life. Still, I found myself

....

lessen the blow make us feel any better

adamant in sticking to their conclusion determined to expel her

have a scholarship to receive money to go to

daydreaming about what it would be like to get on that airplane with her and go to a place where there was no Central High School, no segregationists, and no pain stinging my heart every time someone called me a nigger.

Late one afternoon, a few days before Minnijean was to leave, I sat on the side of her bed, watching her pack. The two of us were talking and giggling. Again I **was overwhelmed with those mixed feelings**. I desperately wanted her to stay, and at the same time I would have given anything to go with her. She was showing me her wardrobe, gifts from friends to help her adjust to her new life. They were the most beautiful clothes I had ever seen: angora sweaters in deep autumn shades of rust and green, with matching corduroy skirts, a few of those wonderful fuzzy collars everyone was wearing, a velvet blazer, and even a beautiful trench coat.

I was so sad I could barely speak, but I was pretending everything was all right and that I was happy for her. What I really wanted to say was I miss you already, I love you like a sister . . . I don't know what I'll do without you. But that would sound too **mushy, so I kept my thoughts to myself**.

Suddenly she slumped down onto the bed amid all those beautiful clothes and her new luggage and started to cry uncontrollably. "I'm really sorry all this is happening. It's going to make it hard for the rest of you."

I tried to console her. "It's not your fault, Minnijean."

"I'll miss you." She embraced me. "I'll miss riding home with you and playing records with you and . . ."

....

was overwhelmed with those mixed feelings had many different feelings

mushy, so I kept my thoughts to myself emotional, so I said nothing

"Yeah, but look at where you're going. New Lincoln High School is a famous place. Those are rich people you're staying with. I'll bet you get your own phone and maybe even a car. You'll meet important people."

"Do you forgive me?"

"There's nothing to forgive. But for the grace of God it might have been any one of us." To distract myself from **the tears welling up inside my heart**, I began folding things to put in her suitcase. "If you don't pack, I get to keep all these gorgeous things and go away and you'll have to stay here in my place," I teased.

With the announcement that Minnijean was definitely out, the segregationists **went wild**. The signs on the walls said: "All niggers go north." An article in the newspaper announced that hall patrols by federalized National Guardsmen would be eliminated, although they would remain in the building and make periodic checks. That announcement granted segregationists more permission to **have a field day with** us. The school days that followed were noted in my diary in terms of the particular **indignities** I suffered. Putting every detail down on paper would give God a chance to see for himself what was going on, I thought.

February 18, 1958.
A red-haired, freckle-faced girl, the one who taunts me in homeroom, keeps trailing me in the hallway between classes.

....

the tears welling up inside my heart how sad I felt
went wild grew even braver
have a field day with do what they wanted to
indignities embarrassments, humiliations

*Today she spit on me, then slapped me. Later in the day as I came around a corner, she tripped me so that I fell down a flight of stairs. I picked myself up to face a group of boys who then chased me up the stairs. When I told a school official about it, he said she was from a good family and would never do such a thing and I needed a teacher to witness these incidents if he were going to take any action. He asked me what did I expect when I came to a place where I knew I wasn't welcome. He warned me **to keep Minnijean's expulsion in mind**.*

February 19

*Andy again. He's really beginning to frighten me. As I **emerged from** the cafeteria today, he walked right up, face to face, stepping on my toes so I couldn't move for a long moment. He shoved me backward and then held a **wrench** up to my face. He waved it around and shouted all sorts of threats that he could do a lot of awful things to my face with it. My knees were shaking and I didn't know what to do. I said, "Thank you." His eyes grew huge. Quicker than the speed of light, I jumped away from him and ran. "Just think all night about what I'm gonna do to you tomorrow," he shouted after me.*

February 20

*I got hit across the back with a tennis racquet. I managed to smile and say, "Thank you." Andy said, "What did you say, nigger?" I repeated, "Thank you very much." I spit up blood in the rest room. I felt as though someone had stuck a hot **poker***

----

to keep Minnijean's expulsion in mind *that I could easily be expelled like Minnijean*

emerged from *came out of*

wrench *heavy metal tool*

poker *metal stick*

through my back, into my insides. I saw him several times during the afternoon, but I never let him see me cry, and I didn't report it to anybody.

I think only the warrior exists in me now. Melba went away to hide. She was too frightened to stay here.

By the beginning of March, I had sunk into the state of mind you get into when you know you have to take castor oil and there's no **way out**. I just did what had to be done, without discussing it or thinking about it. I would get up, polish my saddle shoes, bathe, get dressed, dump my bowl of oatmeal into the toilet so Grandma India would think I'd eaten it—but my nervous stomach wouldn't have to **eject it**—and go to the war inside that school. I listened to shouts, to ugly names, while I smiled and said "Thank you." I waited for a ride, came home, did homework, got to bed, and started over again the next day. I felt kind of numb, as though nothing mattered anymore.

I thought my routine must be like a soldier's fighting in wartime, only I was lucky enough to have weekends **in another world**. One day I was doing just that, thinking about my other world and about the headline I had seen that read: "It's Lovely, Says Minnijean of Her New York School." What would it be like to have just one lovely day of school amid pleasant people who smiled when you looked them in the eye?

As I stood alone outside the Sixteenth Street entrance of Central High, I was shivering against the cold, waiting for my ride home that Friday afternoon. I was **immersed in fantasies**

....

way out other choice
eject it throw it up; vomit
in another world free of attacks
immersed in fantasies thinking

200

about my quiet, safe weekend. My body was there, but my mind was somewhere else.

My 101st guard Danny had said, "When you let yourself lose your focus, you make big mistakes." I suddenly realized that I had done just that, made a foolish mistake. The Sixteenth Street entrance was one of the most dangerous areas of Central High's grounds.

Suddenly there was a voice in the distance, calling my name, jolting me from my thoughts. "It's nigger Melba." It was Andy's voice shouting at me. My heart started beating fast. He was more than a block away, coming up from the playing field with a group of his friends. They were walking fast, almost galloping. Even if I started running, I couldn't **out-distance** all of them. I looked around frantically, searching for help.

"Hey, Melba, you gotta get out of here." The second voice was much closer. I wasn't alone. There was a sleek, muscular boy, about six feet tall, wearing a varsity jacket and a cap, with a bushy shock of blond curls peeking from beneath it. He was leaning against the passenger side of a 1949 Chevy parked at the curb, only a few feet to my left. Was he one of Andy's friends, who'd come to **corner** me and hold me there? His face looked familiar to me. He resembled one of those big tough boys who **got their kicks** taunting me. But why wasn't he coming toward me, shouting ugly words at me like the others?

"Nigger, nigger on the wall, who's the deadest of them all," Andy shouted as he hesitated, waiting for his friends. Now they were only about a quarter of a block away. "Stand still, don't

----

out-distance run away from; avoid
corner trap
got their kicks enjoyed

run, 'cause if you do, **it'll be worse for you**," Andy shouted.

What now? My mind scrambled to figure out what I should do.

"Melba," the blond boy whispered my name, "listen to me. I'm gonna call you nigger—loud. I'm gonna curse at you, but I'm gonna put my keys on the trunk of this car. Get out of here now. My name is Link, I'll call you later."

"But I can't do that."

"Get the hell out of here. . . . Andy's gonna kill you.

"But I can't. . . . I . . . uh . . ." I stood there gasping for words. He's **up to something**, I thought. Now I'm surrounded. Why doesn't the car-pool driver come after me now . . . right now, please, God.

"You don't have any choice," he whispered. "Go!" I turned to see that Andy and his friends were only a short distance away. I wasn't even sure I could make it to the car.

"If you don't get out of here, you're gonna get us both killed," the blond boy urged.

"Hey, Andy, we're gonna have us some nigger tonight." I heard Link shout as he walked away from the car, toward them. I grabbed the keys and ran around quickly to open the door on the driver's side. I hopped in and locked all the doors. By the time I turned the key in the engine, Andy was **clawing at the lock**, while the other boys popped off the windshield wipers, and tried to get into the passenger's side. Link stood glaring at me with an anxious look on his face, spewing hate words just like them. I pressed down the clutch, shifted into first gear,

....

it'll be worse for you we will hurt you more

up to something planning to trick me

clawing at the lock trying to get the door unlocked

and the car jumped forward. Andy was still running alongside, holding on to the door handle, but as I sped up, he had to let go. Even if that boy Link got me later for stealing his car, I was alive and **on my way** for now.

After a couple of blocks, when I could breathe a little easier, I craned to look around. I couldn't see anybody following me. "Thank you, God," I whispered, as I headed for home. "Thank you for saving me one more time."

---

on my way out of danger

BEFORE YOU MOVE ON...

1. **Main Idea and Details** Find 2 entries from Melba's diary that support the main idea: Melba felt she could not endure more attacks.

2. **Problem and Solution** Reread pages 202–203. Andy and his friends chased Melba. How did she get away?

LOOK AHEAD Read pages 204–225 to find out who helped Melba.

15

I gunned the engine of Link's car and began moving as fast as I could without attracting too much attention. By the time I **rounded** the corner at Twelfth and Cross and headed for the backyard, I felt myself going out of control. The car **careened** into our yard. I was moving so fast that I knocked down the fence my uncle Charlie had begun to build around Grandma India's flower garden.

"Have you lost your mind, girl?" Grandma said, wiping her hands on her apron as she held the screen door open and peered into the backyard. "What's going on? Whose car is that?" She was stretching to see past me.

"Uh, it belongs to a school friend. Let me in."

I motioned her to back away and then carefully latched the screen and locked the door behind me. Pulling the curtain back from the glass peephole in the door, I took one last look to see whether or not someone was following me. I started to tell Grandma what happened.

"You mean to tell me that car belongs to some Central High white boy?" She was horrified. I tried to calm her

....

rounded turned
careened sped dangerously
Have you lost your mind What is wrong with you

204

as I explained, but the expression on her face turned from astonishment to fear. Suddenly she hurried to the linen closet and started frantically searching for something. She pulled out several torn and faded sheets and a whole bunch of safety pins. Dragging me with her, she rushed out the back door. We **squared off** the first sheet, holding its corners the way we did to make the big bed in Mama's room, and then pulled it across the hood of the car. "Maybe you'll live to see tomorrow if we can hide this car from the police." She motioned me to help her stretch the second sheet across the roof of the car.

"**I s'pose you were stuck twixt the devil and the deep blue sea, child.** You done your best, but we got us some real trouble now." We rushed into the house and locked the door behind us.

When Mother Lois came home from teaching, she was just as upset as Grandma. After lots of questions and lots of pacing, she calmed down a bit.

"Well, maybe this isn't so bad after all," she said. "It's been a while and nobody's come to **inquire** about the car yet."

Grandma put her hands on Mother's shoulders and said, "Perhaps the boy was telling the truth. Who's to say that he can't be one of God's good white people?"

"I suppose," Mother said as her frown eased a bit. "Let's assume for a moment that this boy wasn't trying to trap you. How are you gonna get the car back to him without other people finding out about it?"

"Link said he'd call," I replied, as I began to search for ways

....

squared off opened

I s'pose you were stuck twixt the devil and the deep blue sea, child. I guess you had no other choice than to take the car.

inquire question us; ask

of returning the car if he didn't. I surely couldn't drive it back to school the next day. He couldn't be seen in my neighborhood, and I dared not travel in his, especially not at night. Well, we would have to figure out a secret way. When the phone rang, I raced to pick up the receiver.

"Hi. It's Link."

"How do I know it's you?"

"My key chain has a little gold football on it."

"Okay. Thank you, Link, thank you very much."

"Andy swears he's gonna get you next time."

"Yeah, he frightens me."

"Look, we better hurry and get this car thing over with. Andy is suspicious that you drove away in my car. I told him no—it's a coincidence that it looked like mine. But I need to make sure he sees me driving my car."

"Whatever you say." I whispered a prayer that Andy hadn't called the police.

"Why don't you drop it off in front of Double Deck Ice Cream. Nobody would **give it a second thought** if we were there at the same time."

"Why did you do it?" **My curiosity was killing me.** I had to ask.

"Because he was real serious about killing you. Don't **take his threats lightly**! He means it! Hey, gotta go—be there in a half an hour."

We couldn't risk asking a neighbor's help, so even though I didn't have a license, I had to drive Link's car downtown. I

---

give it a second thought think it was strange
My curiosity was killing me. I did not understand.
take his threats lightly think he won't try to kill you

wondered what he must be like. The inside of the car was what Conrad called "cherry" clean and polished as if he washed it twice a week. The record albums on the backseat were the same ones I might have chosen—Johnny Mathis, Sam Cooke, Elvis, and Pat Boone. Who was Link, anyhow? Suddenly I felt frightened. Maybe he was a member of the **Klan**—maybe they were waiting with him for me to bring this car back, and they were going to grab me. I concentrated on my driving to get rid of those thoughts.

I pulled up in front of Double Deck Ice Cream. Mama was right behind me. I looked all around to make certain there were no Central students who might recognize me. I parked Link's car at the curb, a little ways down from the front entryway. After leaving the keys beneath the floor mat on the driver's side, I walked back to our car. I couldn't resist taking a quick look around to see if I could spot Link. If he was there I couldn't see him. I climbed into the passenger's side of our car, and we were safely on our way home.

The next day when I saw Andy, he was walking past Mrs. Huckaby's office. There were two other teachers standing nearby, so although he growled at me, threatening that he would get me before the day was over, he kept walking.

Each time I passed Link in the hallway, he winked at me. It was the one kind gesture in a morning filled with hellish activity. In the days that followed, every time I saw Link, he **acknowledged me** in some way. His wink or pleasant expression sometimes came just at the moment I needed to

....

Klan racist organization called the Ku Klux Klan
acknowledged me showed me that he knew me

know I was alive and valuable.

March 23
The AME churches gave the eight of us white Bibles with our names engraved on them during afternoon services. It made me feel like my people are supporting me.

En route to lunch the next day, as I approached my locker, I noticed the door was open; someone had **hammered** the lock and dumped out my books. I had to go to Mrs. Huckaby's office to report the incident. I would need new books for afternoon class, and I would miss being with my friends for the full lunch period.

I walked into the cafeteria, after reporting my loss to Mrs. Huckaby and getting new books, to find that my friends had already left. I wondered why they had left early. Could it be that they had gone to look for me? As I settled down in my seat and began to unwrap the sandwich Grandma had made for me, I noticed a group of boys moving in close to me, much closer than usual. There had always been a wide path of empty chairs immediately surrounding our eating area because other students **shunned** us during the lunch period.

Maybe they felt free to harass me **so openly** because this was one of those days when school officials were experimenting— seeing whether or not we could survive without uniformed federalized troops or school officials posted where everyone could see them. There were no guards in the halls when we

....

hammered broken
shunned avoided, ignored
so openly without being afraid they would get into trouble

changed classes, no guards just outside the cafeteria doors, within shouting distance, as they often were. There were no officials pacing the floor or hugging the walls observing what was going on.

I began to get nervous. I could tell it was no accident that I was being surrounded by the group of sideburners who appeared to have mischievous plans for me. As I looked around, suddenly I saw him. There was Link, seated among my attackers, laughing, joking with them, behaving as though he were a regular member of the group.

I studied him, waiting for his eyes to **catch** mine, and when they did, he looked down quickly. It both frightened and saddened me to see Link among those hoodlums. I stared at him in disbelief and anger. Had he pretended to be a nice person when he was just one of them? I struggled to **regain my composure**. As usual, I was seated near the main entryway, with my back as near to the wall as I could get so that my rear would be protected; but with those boys becoming **more vocally hostile** every moment, and the guards absent, my safe seat seemed to be a trap. I looked off into the distance, where some of my people were serving food from behind the counter. There was no way any of them could help me.

There must have been a thousand or so students in that huge room. It was near the beginning of the second lunch period, a time when the cafeteria was most crowded. Even above the ear-shattering levels of conversation that blended into a **hodgepodge** of unsettling noise, I could hear my attackers'

....

catch look at
regain my composure become calm
more vocally hostile louder and meaner
hodgepodge mixture, combination

comments shouted at me.

Over and over again they were saying how they were going to come and get me, and what they would do with me. I was trying to ignore them, concentrating instead on a plan for my escape, when a milk carton came flying at me, hitting me on the forehead. It was followed by something that pierced my cheek. It took a moment to realize one of the boys had a bean shooter. I flinched, but braced myself so I would not show a reaction, even though the prick was painful.

I ducked down quickly to avoid a hard white object that came whizzing through the air. I **narrowly averted** the missile, and when I reached to examine it, I found a golf ball wrapped in paper. Remembering my discussion with Grandma about playing mind games, I examined it as if it were a **precious** treasure. I smiled and gushed, loud enough for those sitting closest to me to hear. "It's just beautiful, thank you. It's just what I need."

My hecklers began mumbling among themselves. They were far enough away that I couldn't hear exactly what they were saying, but I watched the puzzled expressions on their faces. They looked at me as if I had lost my mind. I glanced at Link to see his reaction. It was hard to **read**. I had to stop wondering about Link and figure out what to do. "Don't do anything," **the voice in my head kept repeating**.

Recently school officials had issued a warning about students who initiated attacks. The penalty was suspension. I suspected that as long as I remained in my seat, no one was going to walk over and dump soup on my head or attack me. With all those

....

narrowly averted barely avoided being hit by
precious great, valuable
read tell what he was thinking
the voice in my head kept repeating I continued to think

other students seated close enough to watch what was going on, my attackers would want it to appear that I made the first move, forcing them to retaliate.

When the bell rang, the room became even more noisy with people shoving chairs, finding their books, and rushing toward the exit. I desperately wanted to get out of there, but I knew I couldn't move or the group would start a fight and set me up for expulsion, for sure. **Word was** they had psychological experts training them in ways of forcing us to respond.

I was willing to sit in that spot **until the end of time** rather than risk a fight. I was already wearing Band-Aids on my heels from the heel-walkers the day before, and I was sore up and down the backs of my legs from being kicked. I felt I couldn't take any more. I knew I couldn't help but fight back against the next person who attacked me.

I pretended to become intensely involved in my book. I was reading about Mr. Gandhi's prison experience and how he quieted his fears and **directed** his thoughts so that his enemies were never really in charge of him.

All at once I was aware that one of my hecklers was coming toward me.

"Niggers are stupid, they gotta study real hard, don't they?" he said in a loud voice.

"Thanks for the compliment," I said, looking at him with the pleasantest expression I could muster so he would believe I wasn't annoyed.

"Study hard now, nigger bitch, but you gotta leave this place

....

Word was People were saying that
until the end of time forever
directed focused

sometime, and then we got you."

"Thank you," I said again, a mask of fake cheer on my face. He seemed astonished as he slowly started to back away.

I felt myself smiling inside. As Grandma India said, **turning the other cheek** could be difficult, but for me, it was also beginning to be a lot of fun. Somehow I had won a round in a bizarre mental contest.

My heart slowed its rapid beating, and my hands stopped shaking. I felt safer, even comfortable, as **something inside me settled to its center.** I had a powerful feeling of being in charge. I was no longer allowing hecklers' behavior to frighten me into acting a certain way. For that moment, I was the one making decisions about how I would behave. A little choir of voices in my head was singing, "Hallelujah, hallelujah, hallelujah!"

The second bell rang for the beginning of the next period; by that time students were expected to be settled into their seats. I saw Link **beckon the hecklers into a huddle**. From the expressions on their faces, I could tell there was serious conversation about what to do next. All at once the group, led by Link, made their way to the door.

"Hey, I'm not gonna stay in detention hall every morning for a week just for a little nigger-beating pleasure," I heard Link say as he passed close by me. I heard them arguing with one another, heard some of them agree that it would be worth it if they could get me once and for all. But I heard Link's voice as he said it was better to leave now and he'd help them get me later for sure.

....

turning the other cheek ignoring them

something inside me settled to its center I calmed down

beckon the hecklers into a huddle gather the mean students into a group to talk to them

16

"I did it," I shouted with excitement as I raced in the front door where Grandma was standing in her usual place to welcome me home after school.

"Did what?" she asked.

"I tried to do some of the things Gandhi talks about—you know, keeping calm in your own mind no matter what's going on outside."

"Phone's for you, Melba," Conrad yelled from the hallway. I hoped it would be someone I could share my victory with, maybe Vince, but it was Link. I slammed the receiver down. Right away the phone started to ring again. I picked up and said, "Don't bother to call again!" I slammed the receiver down once more. Again it rang and rang. Grandma walked into the hallway and eyed me suspiciously. I picked up the receiver for fear of having to explain to her.

"Five minutes, that's all I ask!" Link said. "I **saved your skin**. At least you **owe** me a chance to explain."

"Absolutely not—" I said, but he cut me off before I could finish.

....

saved your skin kept you from getting hurt
owe can give

"I didn't want to be there, but I heard they were gonna do something big to you in the cafeteria. So I thought if I was there I could do something to help you."

"How did you know they were planning something?"

"My dad makes me go to those meetings—where they plan what to do to get you'all kicked out of school."

"Why are you telling me this?"

"Because I want to help you."

"I can't trust you after today."

"Hey, if I hadn't convinced those guys to leave, they were gonna get you. And if you don't believe I'm on your side, here's proof, **listen up**. Stay off the far end of the second floor tomorrow. And don't go to your locker after lunch."

"I gotta go, Grandma wants me." She was standing over me, looking as though she was upset with me.

I rushed to the kitchen with her following on my heels. I had to tell them what had happened, and it was only a matter of minutes before Mother and Grandma **tore into me**. Mother Lois was first to speak. "We have to wonder about Link's motives."

Then Grandma said, "Perhaps he's trying to set you up for the Klan—he's gonna **lure** you into a trap, and then where will you be?"

Although I, too, was undecided about trusting Link, I continued to defend Link as both of them came up with dozens of reasons why I shouldn't trust this white boy. Still, there was something inside me that said he had taken a big risk giving me

listen up pay attention; listen to me
tore into me started yelling at me
lure lead

his car that day.

I didn't want to **defy** Mother and Grandma, but Link was inside Central. He understood what I was going through. They could not help me inside that school. I had no choice but to take any help that would enable me to survive. I had to take the risk of trusting Link a little bit, at least for now.

The next day I **heeded Link's warnings**, taking a different route to class. Later I heard there was trouble on the route I usually took. By not going to my locker in the afternoon, I avoided meeting someone who must have been very angry, as he or she broke the lock and shredded the contents of the locker. The day had gone exactly as Link had said it would, but even so, I found myself wondering if he were only building my trust in order to lay a bigger trap for me.

Link warned me that with the beginning of April, segregationists would feel compelled to speed up their efforts, in order to get us out of Central before we could complete a full school year. Some of their tactics became desperate, and their desperation made it easier for me to avoid the more obvious traps they set.

In the days that followed, Link continued to phone me every night. Grandma India would hand me the receiver with a scowl on her face, but neither she nor Mother Lois forbade my talking with him. Sometimes Grandma even stood by, listening to the entire conversation, with arms folded and a huffy attitude. It was the first time I had ever continued to do something I knew they didn't want me to do. I think Mother finally realized that

....

defy disobey
heeded Link's warning did what Link told me to do

Link was doing something for me they could not do—**feeding me vital** information that could help me survive.

Link **swore me to secrecy**, so other than Mother and Grandmother, none of the other seven students knew he existed. Occasionally, during a general conversation about **do's and don't's**, I would share some information that I thought would be helpful to them, but otherwise I kept my mouth shut. I figured I owed Link that.

After a while, having him as my friend got to be fun for both of us. We played a **cloak-and-dagger** game, passing notes in books and such. But we never spoke to each other in school, or walked near each other, or acknowledged each other except with our eyes for fear he would get caught. He continued hanging around with Andy and his friends and attending the segregationists' strategy meetings. He said the worst part of it for him was that he felt himself a traitor. He was torn between his loyalty to his family and friends, and his sense of guilt and responsibility for what was happening to the eight of us. Sometimes he justified what he was doing by saying if he protected me and prevented a major catastrophe from befalling any of the eight of us, he could insure some of his normal graduation activities, and besides, people wouldn't think Central such an awful place.

Meanwhile, we did indeed notice some stronger efforts by a few teachers to discipline students. The Little Rock School Board now demanded belligerent students be brought under control. At first we saw no difference, but we began to notice

....

feeding me vital telling me important
swore me to secrecy made me promise not to tell anyone
do's and don't's things we should and should not do
cloak-and-dagger secret, mysterious

a slight bit of peace in the hallways, and we were **heartened** to hear that another girl had been expelled for handing out the cards saying "One Down, Eight to Go."

Easter. What a wonderful word, I thought to myself as I walked to Grandma's room. If Easter Sunday was coming soon, it meant the end of school was only weeks away. The twenty-ninth of May. What would that last day of school at Central High be like?

"Tonight's the night," Grandma said, making the announcement from her perch in her favorite chair. "We're going into the trunks tonight. It's time to make your selections." She smiled with her all-knowing expression, because she was fully aware of how much it delighted us to view and touch her trunk treasures. There were **gifts, heirlooms, and mementos** we got to touch or see only at Christmas or Easter.

There they were in the center of the room, the old trunks given to Grandma India as a young girl. One was a deep brown, with scrapes and scratches visible beneath the glossy **veneer** she kept up with biannual waxing. The second one was a deep garnet color and looked newer.

"Have you given much thought to what you'll be wearing to church this Easter, Melba?" Grandma India asked as she lifted the lid of the first trunk.

I had thought long and hard about wanting to dress grown-up. The strength growing inside me to face the hostile students at Central had **leaked into my home life**. Now it bubbled up

....

heartened glad, encouraged
gifts, heirlooms, and mementos special things
veneer surface
leaked into my home life become a part of me

in me, allowing me to speak my mind. "I'd like to wear nylon stockings and little heels with whatever I wear. I am sixteen now, sixteen and a half, actually." It was a daring suggestion, considering Grandma's opinions on the subject.

"Nylon stockings—heels. Have you been reading those trashy fashion magazines again? Let's not move too fast, young lady. You've got all your life to wear stockings, but you'll only be young once." Grandma seemed adamant about my remaining a two-year-old, I thought to myself. It was the only thing she and Papa Will agreed on. He thought wearing nylon stockings and dating should begin at age twenty, but since he didn't live with us, I knew what he thought wouldn't have to be the rule for what happened in my life. But Grandma was right there, keeping me from growing up. Nevertheless, as she fussed and fumed about my **wicked desires**, I kept my expression pleasant, the same as I did in the halls of Central High in order to avoid expulsion.

"Let's take some time to think about the stockings," Mother Lois said, smiling and moving toward the trunk to peek inside. "Tonight we'll pick our special cloth from the trunks and get going on a design for all of our dresses and for Conrad's shirt."

"Lois, maybe **something two-piece** would be nice for Melba this year," Grandma said.

Mama and Grandma would draw a picture, then sit in the middle of the floor and cut a pattern out of newspaper, and make a dress **come to life in** the fabric.

For the next hour, we **rummaged** through Grandma's trunks

....

wicked desires wanting to dress like a grown up
something two-piece a skirt and a blouse
come to life in using
rummaged looked, searched

filled with fabrics she had collected over the years. There were remnants of dresses and suits I had seen her wear all my life. There were brand-new pieces and full **bolts** she had gotten from her mother before she died or from her sisters as trades for other things. Easter was always a time when we each were allowed to choose the cloth we wanted.

Celebrating the Easter holiday was a big event in our family. Attending church on Easter was a grand ceremony when everybody dressed up in the very best they could afford. There was always an Easter-egg hunt on the church grounds, and a parade of people in special hats. A few weeks back we had officially begun the sacred holiday with the pledge of our sacrifices for Lent. It was a family tradition that Mama and Grandma would review our Lenten commitment as we shopped the trunks.

"Have you two considered adding more items to your sacrifice list this year?" Grandma asked as she began to sketch the design for my dress.

"Uh, Grapette colas. That's what I'm doing without. I haven't **slipped** yet," I declared, remembering how many times I'd thought about slipping.

"That's all?" Grandma's tone let me know she wasn't pleased with either the number or quality of sacrifices on my list. One year I had chosen to give up the radio, and another, candy bars. I knew for sure I would never promise to give up either of those things again.

"Well, what about giving up television to spend more time

....

bolts rolls of fabric
slipped broken my promise

reading your Bible?" Grandma said.

"Ohhhh, Mother, Grandma, please, since I'm giving up so much in Central, can't you let me **slide by** this year?" I pleaded with them as I sat caressing the thick folded piece of purple velvet I had pulled from the trunk.

"There's lots of hard work to be done on **repenting** for sins. Have you listed your sins?" As Grandma spoke, she rocked back and forth a little faster, and turned her attention away from her sketching to look at me.

"I've lumped together into one big sin all the hundreds of times I thought evil of people at Central," I said. "There were also several times I thought about **sassing adults back**, mostly teachers and principals at school. And I didn't trust God on two occasions."

"And how about not answering all your fan mail?" Mother Lois added. "Don't you think it a sin to ignore all those people who take their valuable time to write to you? You were so good about it at first."

I realized she was right. At the beginning, I had faithfully answered those letters each weekend. They came from France, Germany, England, Africa, and Australia, from people all around the world, mostly congratulating me for going to Central High. Grandma would **sift** out the mean ones, which were few and far between. I got several marriage proposals from cute boys, some of them white, who sent their pictures. Grandma forbade me to send them more than a polite thank-you. I wanted at least to learn more about them and file them

....

slide by not give up as much
repenting asking God for forgiveness
sassing adults back being rude to an adult
sift take

in an "if you need a husband when you're a grown-up" file. But Grandma said that would be a personal sin.

Late one evening Link telephoned. He was furious about the announcement of the cancellation of many of his senior class activities. He spoke of all his hard work to maintain good grades, his athletic awards, and his student leadership, and now his hopes for a wonderful senior year were dashed. The traditional senior events had been canceled because of the possibility of trouble as a result of integration. School officials also cited the presence of the Arkansas National Guard as another reason.

Link was **inconsolable**. "I don't know what I can do about it," I said even as I wondered whether his disappointment and anger would make him **turn against** me.

"You can do a news interview saying we're not such bad people and that everything is getting better at school. That way everybody in the world won't think we're all **villains**."

"Link, you don't want me to lie, do you? Everything is getting worse, not better."

On and on he went, telling me how Central High's students were suffering and **sacrificing** the reputation of their nationally acclaimed school because we had come there. He was more angry than I'd ever heard him. "This was a good school, ranked high on the national scale, and now our halls are filled with soldiers and people are treating us like criminals!"

I could only think to tell him to have faith that God would

....

inconsolable not comforted by anything I said
turn against hate
villains bad people
sacrificing giving up

make things okay. I couldn't do what he asked; I couldn't change things. That's when he really got sarcastic, saying, "Don't give me that God stuff. That's what Nana Healey always says. I don't believe in God. If he's there, why is he letting all this happen?"

"Who's Nana Healey?"

"My nanny. She's **colored**—like you." He had often spoken of her, but this was the first time he had told me she was not white.

"The reason I'm attending Central is so I don't have to spend my life being somebody's nanny," I said in a tone to match his indignant manner.

By the end of the conversation, Link's anger had shifted from me to the situation. He was frustrated, vowing he was going to do something about the cancellation. Our conversation **aroused my suspicions anew**. Was he just being nice to me temporarily to get me to lie to the news people? Who was he? After all, I had no way of **checking him out**. I couldn't tell the others about him or talk about him to the NAACP people. I was at his mercy, having to decide on my own whether or not he was genuine. I would have to be on constant alert from now on, watching for signs of what his real motives were.

But meanwhile he warned me to watch out for any students who tried to hand me election pamphlets. School officers were to be elected on April 24. Students would be nice and offer us literature, he said, but as we paused to take it they would ink our dress, grab our books, or worse. "I've been to some of those planning meetings recently, and I can tell you they're **gonna pull out all stops** and do everything they can to get you out of

....

colored African American
aroused my suspicions anew made me not trust him
checking him out finding out what others knew of him
gonna pull out all stops not going to stop for any reason

school before it ends, to make certain you're not coming back next year."

"What more could they do? They're already exhausting us."

"Yeah, but it's gonna get much worse. The thing is, lately they've been talking about pulling off something really big that will not only hurt you but your families—something that will force you to quit."

Back at school on Monday, just as Link had warned, people approached us as though they were including us in the election process. They would offer a pamphlet with one hand while using the other hand to shower us with all manner of smelly liquids. Sometimes they would kick or even punch us, and usually whatever they did was followed by rude name-calling.

The elections at our old school, Horace Mann, weren't nearly so **sophisticated**. At Central, people put up signs, wore buttons, and passed out materials, just as though it were a real election. They held **debates** and voting parties and did all manner of campaigning. I was intrigued watching the process, delighted at the complexity of it all compared to what I had been accustomed to at our old school. It made me extra sad that I wasn't allowed to **participate**.

More frequently now Link was full of talk about graduation events. Under any other circumstances, this would have been an exciting time of year, filled with wonderful events. He told me about the parties for the juniors and seniors. He told me about a huge **gala** at the Marion Hotel, and said the junior and senior picnics at Central High were better than Christmas and New

---

sophisticated detailed, complicated
debates talks between candidates
participate be a part of it
gala celebration, party

Year's combined. It made me feel more isolated, because now I was also left out of the events at my old high school.

As our conversations grew more relaxed, Link began telling me about his parents. His father, a wealthy and very well-known businessman, had been forced to contribute money to the Citizens Council campaign in order to do a healthy amount of business in Little Rock. "He isn't for race mixing, but he also isn't for beating up anybody's children," Link explained.

JUDGE LEMLEY TO HEAR SCHOOL BOARD'S PETITION
—*Arkansas Gazette*, Tuesday, April 22, 1958

As I read the article I felt **despair creeping over me**. Judge Harry Lemley of Hope, Arkansas, had been **named to hear** the Little Rock School Board petition asking for a **postponement** of integration for public schools. The first hearing was set for the following Monday at 9:30 A.M. He promised the final hearing would be held long before September. The article described him as a native of Upperville, Virginia, and a man who "loved the South as though it were a religion." It was evident from that description that he wouldn't be likely to **violate** southern tradition for my people.

I desperately needed the break that came with the Easter holiday. As usual on Easter Sunday morning, each of us twirled and pranced in our family fashion show. "Spiffy do," Grandma

....

despair creeping over me very sad
named to hear chosen to judge
postponement delay
violate change

India said as we climbed into the car. The church was filled to the rafters with people we didn't see during all the rest of the year.

Vince and I sat together at the church dinner, reminiscing about our earlier dates, and for the first time I felt as though we were good friends again. Still, he was not someone with whom I could talk about my Central High experience. We **had simply drifted apart** because we had so little in common, except our past relationship.

In my diary I wrote:

> *I am happy today, but I am also frightened.* **The appointment of Lemley** *means we have to pray hard. This is not supposed to happen in America. I mean segregationists aren't supposed to be able to have their own judge.*
>
> *I salute the flag every morning as I look at a picture on the homeroom wall directly in front of me. I will never forget that picture as long as I live. It is a brown pasture with white sheep. As the boys behind me call names and the girls to each side* **sneer***, I look straight ahead because those sheep are smiling at me. I think it is a smile from God. It is a promise that if I salute the flag like a good American, all these integration problems will be worked out eventually.*

....

had simply drifted apart were not close friends anymore

The appointment of Lemley *Lemley being named judge*

sneer *give me mean looks*

BEFORE YOU MOVE ON...

1. **Conclusions** Reread pages 215–216 and 222–223. How did Link help Melba? What did he help her to understand?

2. **Cause and Effect** Reread pages 211–212. What happened when Melba reacted differently to the harassment?

LOOK AHEAD Read pages 226–235 to find out why Link wanted to help Melba.

17

Inside Central, everyone who wasn't talking about getting us out of school seemed to be talking about the upcoming **production of** *The Mikado*. I listened intently for every little crumb of information I could get. I felt **a vicarious** delight just being near the excitement. From what I could learn, the production was nearly professional, with many props and fancy equipment I'd never even heard of. How I longed to be included or at least permitted to attend. I thought I had resigned myself to being left out, but **it was haunting me again**.

The segregationists' campaign against us seemed to get even worse during that week. Sign-carrying, card-dispensing, tripping, kicking crusaders revved up their efforts to reduce our number to zero. Meanwhile Mrs. Huckaby, the woman I considered to be somewhat near fair and rational about the whole situation, had lapsed back into her attitude of trying to convince me there was nothing going on. It seemed as though whenever I reported anything to her, she would **work herself up into a lather**: I was seeing things; was I being too sensitive; did I have specific details?

....

production of play
a vicarious like I shared in the
it was haunting me again I still wanted to belong
work herself up into a lather get very upset

When she stopped behaving in a reasonable way, she took away the only **point of reference** I had. I desperately tried to understand how such an intelligent woman could be reasonable and understanding one moment, then seem so cold, distant, and dispassionate the next. I supposed that she must be under **an enormous weight** and doing her best. I tried to see the overall picture—to remember that over the long haul, she had been a tiny pinpoint of light in the otherwise very dark experience of dealing with Central High's administration. But once again I had to accept the fact that I shouldn't be wasting my time or energy hoping anyone would listen to my reports. I was on my own.

By the end of that week I had flashed endless smiles in response to negative deeds or words. If God was giving stars in crowns in heaven, as Grandma always promised, I'd earned two or three.

By Saturday morning, as my family rushed about the house making breakfast and doing household chores, I lay with my face down in my pillow, hoping they would be quiet. But it was not to be. I had an early morning phone call from Link.

"I need your help," he said. "I want you to come with me now."

"You're crazy. You know we can't be seen together."

"It'll be okay. I promise. I'm going where it'll be safe."

"Where?" I asked.

"You'll see. Meet me on the other side of the bridge—just inside North Little Rock."

....

point of reference help at school

an enormous weight a lot of pressure

I was confused about meeting him. I wondered whether or not this was the trap the **KKK** asked Link to set for me so they could get rid of me.

"Please, Melba," he pleaded. Hearing the urgency in his voice I decided to do what he wanted. I felt queasy as I explained to Mama and Grandma that there was a big emergency with Thelma and I was going to visit her. It was the first time in my life I had ever looked them in the eye and told **an untruth**. They were reluctant to let me go, but I promised I would stay in our own neighborhood, where it was safe. I prayed for God's forgiveness for lying as I drove away.

I spotted Link's car just on the North Little Rock side of the bridge. In broad daylight I parked my car and got into his. He told me we were going to Nana Healey's house. I didn't say much as we drove along. It felt **awkward** being with him. Although we had talked lots on the telephone, he was in some ways a stranger—a white stranger. Sitting next to him made me wonder again who he was and what he wanted with me. I tried to close my mind to Grandmother's words: "The only thing a white man ever wants with one of our women is **personal favors**."

The neighborhood got more and more dismal. It was a part of town where our people lived in awful, run-down chicken-shack houses, some in such bad condition that they looked as though they'd fall down any moment. Folks stood around in clusters, talking. There were groups of men dressed in ragged, filthy clothing, drinking from liquor bottles as they chatted.

....

KKK Ku Klux Klan
an untruth a lie
awkward strange, weird
personal favors to have sex with them

I'd seen places like this before on those rare occasions when Grandma and I passed through as we went to visit friends or our relatives in North Little Rock. Being there made me feel so **fortunate** that Mother had her teaching job. Without that job, I might very well be living in a place like this.

"Hey, why so quiet?" Link touched my arm, and I turned to face him.

"I'm frightened, I guess."

"I'm not gonna let anything happen to you. You're a lot safer here than inside Central, aren't you."

We pulled into the yard of one of the **shabbier** places. I wanted to turn and run. Instead, Link opened the door and reached for my hand as I stepped out into a puddle of water. He teased me about being graceful and having shaky ice-cold hands as I watched him fumble with the key to the trunk.

"Well, don't just stand there, grab a bag." He was pulling bag after bag of groceries out of the trunk and stacking them on the hood of the car. "She hasn't got any **kin**, so I've got to keep her fed."

"Why you? Where are her own people?" I grabbed two bags of food and followed as he led the way.

"She hasn't got any people. She worked for my family all her life. As a young girl, she worked for my grandparents. When Daddy got married, Grandmother sent her to him as a kind of gift. She's been with me all my life."

"Why isn't she with your family anymore?"

" 'Cause she got sick—real sick. My folks **let her go**, just like

....

fortunate lucky
shabbier dirtier and more worn out
kin family
let her go fired her

that, after all the time she'd been so good to us. She's got no money for a doctor. She won't take my money. I think she's got **tuberculosis**. But I don't know for sure." He knocked on the weather-beaten door.

"Nana, it's me. May I come in?" His voice was loud but ever so gentle as he called out to her. A **feeble** voice called back. Holding bags of groceries in his arms, he pushed open the door with his elbow.

There in a dark room sat an aged woman, her **profile etched** against the sun shadow in the one window of the room. Long silver-gray hair in braids framed her lined face, which was worn and weary. Wrinkled skin was stretched taut over protruding cheekbones. Her fingers were stiffened into position as though she were holding an apple, but her hands were empty.

As I moved closer I could see she was wearing a freshly starched, flowered cotton dress just like my own grandmother might have worn. Her appearance was **immaculate**, her posture was erect, and she tilted her chin upward, demonstrating her own dignity and pride despite her circumstances.

The tiny, bare shack was spotlessly clean. It was one room with a makeshift bathroom in plain view. In one corner there was a cracked sink, over which a slab of a broken mirror hung. Despite the run-down condition of the few pieces of furniture and the torn curtains on the window, there were touches of pride all around. A picture frame on her night table held a photo of a small boy with blond curls. Link as a child, I thought.

....

tuberculosis a serious lung disease

feeble weak

profile etched shape could be seen

immaculate absolutely clean

"Nana, I want you to meet my friend Melba," Link said, raising his voice to an ear-shattering level. Then he leaned over to whisper to me, "She can't hear good, go closer. I want you to convince her to see a doc, somebody you know and trust."

"Your friend?" said Mrs. Healey.

"Yes, ma'am, she's my friend, aren't you, Melba?" He was talking loudly and grinning at me as though he wasn't certain of what I would say.

I didn't say anything, turning instead to read Mrs. Healey's reaction. Her expression was angry. She could barely move about or speak, but she gathered her strength, and after a long moment she said, "Boy, you'all are gonna get yourselves in a heap of trouble. **You know better.**"

"Yes, Nana." He knelt beside her and took her hand. "Don't you worry about it. I'll handle it. You talk to Melba while I make a cup of tea for you." He took off his jacket, rolled up his sleeves, and began putting the groceries away. I watched as he placed **staples** in the splintered wood cabinet and on the sagging but meticulously lined shelves above the sink. He behaved as though he had performed those same tasks many times before.

"Mrs. Healey, you're looking very nice today." I drew near to her.

"Well, I don't feel so good. But I gets up and dresses myself. **Cleanliness is next to Godliness.**" Suddenly her **emaciated** body was racked with a cough. She reached for the handkerchief tucked in her sleeve. On and on she coughed. Link turned from

---

You know better. You know you should not be together.

staples necessary food

Cleanliness is next to Godliness. It is important to be clean.

emaciated skinny, thin

his chores, staring at her with a pained expression on his face. He reached for a cup from the cupboard and filled it with water. Holding it up to her mouth, he gently helped her to drink from it.

"Nana, we gotta get you to see a doc." He nudged me with his elbow. "Your turn," he whispered to me.

"Mrs. Healey, this sounds like the kinda cough that isn't going away real soon unless you get some doctoring and the right medicine."

"Oh, I'll be fine," she said, clearing her throat. "Jus' takes a while for me to **get my bearings after one of these spells**." Her voice was raspy, and the coughing started again. On and on she coughed, her feeble body shaking as I tried to hold on to her.

Link got a cold cloth. I held it to her head, and the coughing finally stopped. I made up my mind I was going to help Link get a doctor to come to see her.

After a while, he went back to his work. He opened the door to the icebox. The wheezing old appliance, without light, looked as though the inside panels were ready to fall. It was empty until he started packing shelf after shelf.

"**Wolf was about to get you**, Nana," he said. "You're running kinda short." They giggled to each other as though they understood without speaking.

We spent the rest of the morning with Mrs. Healey. She coughed continuously as we went about our chores. Link again urged me to convince her to take money for a doctor. He said I

....

get my bearings after one of these spells recover
Wolf was about to get you You were about to starve

could tell her it was a loan from the church. I agreed. Watching him tend to Mrs. Healey, I would never again have reason to question his motives.

There was silence between us for a long time as we drove away. Then I couldn't help asking, "And why didn't your folks **make some provision** for her?"

"Whenever I ask my folks, my father turns me off by saying I'm weak—that **I'm a you-know-what lover**. He says colored folks are used to doing without, and I ought not spoil them."

I found a doctor in our community who did not know Mother Lois or Grandma India and asked him to go to Mrs. Healey's. When I spoke with the doctor later, he said there was not a lot he could do for Nana Healey except make her comfortable. What she really needed was long-term care in a hospital. I asked if she was dying, and he told me yes. One of the hardest things I ever had to do was tell Link. There were tears in his voice as he spoke through a rush of anger.

"Damn my folks. They didn't even pay **social security for her**. She's got nothing. I share my allowance with her, and some of the folks in her church give her a few pennies. But they've got nothing like what it will take for a hospital. I've gotta go now. I'll take care of it."

I decided that I had to tell Grandma India about Nana Healey. It took time, but Grandma got over her anger at my disobedience, and sure enough, she promised to visit Mrs. Healey on her weekly trips to North Little Rock. So in the end

....

make some provision set aside some money

I'm a you-know-what lover I love African Americans

social security for her taxes that would allow her to receive checks from the government

Link and Grandma formed something of a friendship as they discussed all the tasks surrounding Nana Healey's care which **compelled** them to get to know each other.

In the days that followed, we were repeatedly warned that nothing mattered more than avoiding any activity that would get us expelled. Now the hoodlums were **mounting a last-ditch** effort to get us out of school before May 29. They wanted no possibility that we could register for the next school term.

Meanwhile Link seemed nervous, asking me each day what had happened. He kept **harping on** the fact that he was hearing that segregationists were going to do something to somebody's family. "Something big that will be certain to get one or more of you guys to voluntarily leave school," he said.

But as the days passed, I was less concerned about Link's warning and more worried about the boy who now came into study hall each day threatening to toss me out of the window, and the girls who encircled me at least once a day, saying every negative thing they could about the parts of my body. Fat thighs, ugly hair, ugly clothing, funny eyes, all shouted in a chorus. I thought sadness would force the tears in my heart to flow, but I never said a word.

At the same time I was worried about Mother Lois, who was becoming more tense with each day. At dinner she hardly spoke. She seldom laughed and didn't offer any of her **corny** jokes. It was a Monday evening when Mother gathered us in

....

compelled forced
mounting a last-ditch organizing one last desperate
harping on repeating, emphasizing
corny silly

the living room for a family conference. I had never seen such a **grave** expression on her face.

"They're not going to renew my teaching contract for next year. I don't have a job," she told us.

"But why?" we all asked. We knew very well that there was no reason to fire her. They couldn't possibly fire her for doing a bad job. She had fourteen years of teaching experience with lots of awards **to her credit**. There were no complaints in her record.

And then with tears brimming in her eyes, she explained. "They say they'll give me back my job only if I **withdraw Melba from** Central High School immediately. They do not want her to finish the year."

---

grave serious, unhappy
to her credit for her work
withdraw Melba from take Melba out of

BEFORE YOU MOVE ON...

1. **Assumption** Reread page 233. What did Link's parents assume about Nana Healy?

2. **Cause and Effect** Reread page 235. Why did Mother Lois lose her teaching job?

LOOK AHEAD Read pages 236–261 to find out how the governor stopped integration.

18

"We have no choice. We have to take the risk talking to newspaper people. Who is going to feed us and put a roof over our heads if I don't get my job back?" Mother Lois's face was tear-stained, but her expression **reflected** the determination I heard in her voice. We sat around the big, old mahogany table in the dining room, discussing a plan to save her job.

"Those segregationists will stop at nothing to get what they want." Grandma appeared angry and anxious as she spoke.

During the last few days of April, Mother Lois had **humbled herself** to make several trips to North Little Rock's school headquarters to plead for her job, but they had refused to **reinstate** her. On five different occasions, her superiors told her they were taking away her contract because she had allowed me to participate in the integration of Central.

Already Mr. Henson had called about our late house payment on the first **mortgage**. The bank was calling about the car. Mother didn't want to plead for any more credit at the grocery store, so the cupboards held a sparse supply of staples. The refrigerator shelves were almost bare. Grandma India was

....

reflected showed
humbled herself ignored her pride and decided
reinstate rehire
mortgage loan

preparing more stews and casseroles with less meat and lots of rice and potatoes. She was dividing one chicken so it stretched into three full meals by using the back and wings in her lemon-rice soup. She was baking plain white bread instead of buying it at the store.

"Sitting and wishing never made man great. **The good Lord sends the fishing, but we gotta dig the bait.** I say we've got to force the hand of those administrators. They're ignoring you." There was fire in Grandma's eyes as she spoke.

The loss of Mama's teaching position had upset all the members of our family. Thinking about it, talking about it, planning for it had taken us up like an Arkansas tornado that pounded and pounded us in the wind. Now my home life was completely taken over by the same tense fretting and worrying as my school life had been. It had happened without warning. Mother explained how the administrator had called her into his office and told her he had the connections to see that she got offered a job in Oklahoma. "Your contract here with us will not be renewed. The job in Oklahoma is your only option," he said.

"But why? I've done a good job here. There have never been any complaints from parents or from this administration."

"This is just one of those things that happens, Mrs. Pattillo. It has nothing to do with the **caliber** of your work. It's simply that we've been ordered to hire a different kind of teacher." He paused. "Of course, there is one way you can keep your job."

"Yes, sir?"

"If Melba were to withdraw from that school, we could talk

··

The good Lord sends the fishing, but we gotta dig the bait. God will provide, but we have to do the work.

caliber quality

about renewing your contract this year at quite a **handsome** salary increase," he said.

Mother was certain he was being pressured by his bosses, North Little Rock's all-white school administrators who were fighting integration in that city. Still, she had not expected **such harsh retaliation**. As she walked away from his office, she recalled what Link had said, "Something bad will happen, something involving the whole family."

As we sat mulling over our fate, I realized that the segregationists had taken away the one thing we couldn't do without—Mama's job. If there was anything that could cause me to leave school, it would be to get Mama's job back.

Grandma was soft-spoken, calm, but emphatic as she said, "Well, Lois, you've tried every polite and proper way of getting that job back. I think some sort of drastic action is called for."

"I don't know . . ." Mother pondered the idea in silence. I had watched her expression become a little more **drawn** with each passing day.

"We could call some of those reporters. The main goal would be to get a story in the local white papers," Grandma said.

"I guess we've got no choice. I've thought about it and prayed about it," Mama finally said. "Tomorrow morning I'm going to write down a paragraph or two and call some of those news people."

There was lots of excitement for the next few days in school as the yearbooks were distributed. Some of our regular

---

handsome big, generous
such harsh retaliation that she would be fired because Melba was integrating
drawn hopeless

adversaries complained loud and long about how the inclusion of some of our pictures had tainted their precious yearbook. But as they became preoccupied with exchanging autographs, a few of them **let up on** chasing and taunting us.

We continued to hear **snippets** of the fancy plans for Central students to have fun during the final weeks of the school year, plans that we could only **speculate** about. Certainly none of the eight of us received even one social invitation, nor could we have risked attending even if we had. To make matters worse, I did not receive any graduation celebration invitations from my old school. At first I had deeply resented being left out, especially since all of us were making huge sacrifices that would benefit everyone in the future. But after thinking about it, I realized that sometimes we were excluded not as an act of hostility but because they had forgotten about us since we weren't visible in their lives anymore.

Over the next few days, I was anxious to get the newspaper to see if somebody would print the story about Mama's job loss. I had watched her go through the awkward ordeal of phoning news people. Three of them listened patiently as she read her two paragraphs explaining the situation. They called back later with questions, and one man interviewed her.

On Wednesday morning, May 7, I was awakened by the slam of the front door and Mother Lois calling out to us from the living room. "It's here. The newspaper did it—they printed the article about my losing my job!"

---

adversaries enemies
let up on stopped
snippets a little talk
speculate wonder

"CHS Crisis Cost Her Job, Says North Little Rock Negro Teacher," the headlines read. The article stated our problem precisely as Mother had told the reporter: The North Little Rock School District had refused to renew her contract to teach seventh-grade English because of her participation in the integration issue.

"Praise the Lord, we got us some power now," Grandma shouted. It was the first time in days I saw hope in everybody's eyes, hope that we could fight all those high-powered white men who were taking Mama's job away.

The phone started to ring. One after another, the calls came. We raced for the telephone, delighted with the people saying they were on our side. Only a few people said negative things, like Mother deserved to lose her job for being **too uppity**. But some of those who wished us well were people calling from other cities. The **wire services had teletyped** the story around the country. People from everywhere promised they'd call the administrator's office and say it was an awful thing to take Mama's job away.

It had been the best morning in many days. We actually laughed over the breakfast table. That good feeling lingered as I entered the front door of Central and climbed the stairs to my third-floor homeroom.

"You better pack your rags and get on outta here, nigger. Your mama's lost her job. What you gonna do now?" The **baiting** went on for most of the morning. They had all read the paper, too. I wondered if it had been one of their parents

···

too uppity proud, arrogant

wire services had teletyped national news services had printed

baiting insults, taunting

who caused Mama to lose her job.

Just as Link had warned, the segregationists were **heating up their campaign** to prevent Ernie, who was a senior, from graduating. They were already saying they were sure we wouldn't be coming back next year because we'd never last through the semester. I could tell that Mrs. Huckaby also sensed real trouble, because she summoned us one by one to discuss our problems.

Until that time, I had been observing fewer and fewer Arkansas National Guard troops inside school each day. It was said they were mostly not on the school grounds but **"on call as the situation warranted."** There had been days in late April when no guards were visible to us in the hallways. But lately, as tension increased, we were aware of them in the building. As those days of May brought more and more physical punishment, for the first time in four months I was assigned a personal bodyguard to follow me from class to class.

However, I never really felt protected by the **insolent-looking, boyish grown-up** who wore the sneer of a brooding Elvis. The soldiers' loyalties were not to us. They made that very clear in their words and deeds.

As we faced days of **grueling** punishment, I was also coping with the fact that despite the newspaper article, we had heard no word from the North Little Rock school administrators about Mama's job. I was bringing sandwiches made of apple butter on bread ends to school for lunch. One of Grandmother's

---

heating up their campaign trying even harder
"on call as the situation warranted" available if needed
insolent-looking, boyish grown-up angry guard
grueling long and awful

friends had given us a basket of apples, so there was apple strudel, apple pie, apple butter, baked apples, and apple jelly.

"We haven't **exhausted all our blessings**. We haven't knocked on the Lord's door the right way," Grandma concluded. So she and Mama decided the next step would be to go to the **presiding bishops** of our community's churches. One of the most powerful of our people was Bishop O. J. Sherman. He told Mother to go back to the white administrator and say one simple sentence: "Bishop Sherman asked me to tell you he would like me to have a job."

Mother did as she was told. The administrator stared down at the papers on his desk, silent, ignoring her for an uncomfortably long moment while he picked the lint off his trousers. "Oh, he did, did he?" He looked up into my mother's eyes, a slight smile creeping onto his face. "Mrs. Pattillo, you don't like the idea of working in Oklahoma, do you?"

"No, sir," she said, speaking firmly.

"I read the articles about you in the newspapers, and we've gotten a lot of calls. Now you've gone and **riled up** the bishops from your community."

"Yes, sir." Mama's tone let him know she meant business.

"Got anything else in mind?"

"Yes, sir. I've got to do whatever it takes to keep my job, because I've got to feed my family. I'm a woman alone. Besides, I've done nothing wrong. I've been a very good teacher all these years. I don't deserve to be treated like this."

The administrator dismissed her politely without saying

---

exhausted all our blessings tried everything
presiding bishops powerful leaders
riled up angered, excited

another word. The next day, when Mama got to school, her boss came to her classroom and congratulated her on her fine teaching abilities. "It'll be nice having you back here next year," he said.

"**I assume your accolades will be forthcoming in writing**," Mama replied. The next afternoon she arrived home carrying her contract. She sat down at the kitchen table and handed it to Grandma, who was placing the dinner plates on the table. Tears streamed down Mama's cheeks as she wrung her hands together to stop their shaking.

"Let's hold hands and pray," Grandma India said. "Praise you, Lord. I knew you wouldn't forget us."

As I marked the May days off my calendar, I felt as though I was caught up in a whirlwind. Ernie was rehearsing for graduation. At the same time, there was a constant shower of threats about stopping him from graduating. Using new tactics, with more frequent attacks that involved more people, the segregationists watched and followed us constantly, looking for ways to **isolate us**.

"You'all think you're gonna have a graduation, but a funeral is what you're really gonna have—no, more like eight funerals." The voice was familiar. Of course, it was my persistent attacker, the ever-present Andy, who continued his threats to get me, no matter what. He had **taken to** chasing me from the gymnasium through the dark walkway that connected it to the main building. He suddenly began backing up his threats by waving

....

I assume your accolades will be forthcoming in writing
I expect that you will have a new contract for me soon

isolate us get us alone

taken to started

a bone-handled switchblade knife in the air. My Arkansas National Guard protector calmly looked on as Andy chased me, getting so close with his knife blade that the book I held up to protect me got slashed through the cover.

"Hey, boy, you could get us into real trouble if you keep that up. You've had your fun, now you gotta move on," the Guardsman said with a **twisted** smile, his cold eyes looking at me as though he would much rather have let Andy **have his way with me**. I stood there trembling, wishing for Danny. My heart was pounding, but I consoled myself with the knowledge that pretty soon I wouldn't have to deal with Andy. Only a few days remained before school would be out. I decided to **duck out of** gym class, vowing I would never walk that way again.

CENTRAL HIGH SCHOOL NEGROES PASS: ONE ON HONOR ROLL. PRINCIPAL MATTHEWS SAYS HE WILL NOT REVEAL GRADES BUT CONFIRMS GREEN WILL GRADUATE.
—*Arkansas Gazette*, Wednesday, May 23, 1958

"We ain't gonna let no nigger wear our cap and gown," one boy shouted at me as I walked the hallway to English class. I pushed my way past him, flashed a smile and a pleasant "Thank you."

At home the phone calls were coming fast and vicious. "We got a way of gettin' you darkies now, for certain. We're offering ten thousand dollars for your **head on a platter**." I gulped as I

....

twisted sick, evil
have his way with me hurt me
duck out of skip, miss
head on a platter death

replaced the receiver in its cradle. I couldn't help thinking about how that was an awful lot of money. Poor folks might **take a notion to collect**. They'd get ten thousand dollars for my head. Did that mean they'd have to cut it off to collect? I told Grandma India of my fears.

"Surely you've got something better to do besides speculating about white folks' silliness," she said.

"I can't help worrying about Ernie. One of those students could **be an impostor**—anybody could wear a robe."

"Impostor?" Grandma looked up from her needlework with a question.

"You know, someone from the KKK who wants to collect that reward money could pretend to be a graduate."

"I don't think Ernie is in any real danger during graduation because he'll be there among six hundred and one white graduates. Besides, God's watching after Ernie just like he's watching over you."

"But . . ." I tried to continue **being in my pity pot**. She motioned me to shush my mouth and hold my hands out so she could circle the embroidery thread around them to straighten it out. After a long moment she said, "You're fretting a mighty lot this evening. Hard work is always the cure for worry. So busy yourself doing those dishes and getting ready for your final exams."

I had always imagined that my last day of the **term** at Central High School would be marked by a grand ceremony,

---

take a notion to collect do it for the money
be an impostor really be a killer
being in my pity pot feeling sorry for myself
term school year

with a massive choir singing hallelujah, or perhaps some wonderful award from my community—a parade maybe. I imagined the roar of helicopters overhead towing flying banners of congratulations—something—anything. But it was just the same as any other day. Four of us, Thelma, Elizabeth, Jeff, and I, rode home together early that afternoon. We wouldn't be going back to Central High for at least three months. Long spaces of silence **punctuated** our talk about how we thought we did on our exams.

"It's over," Conrad said, greeting me as I climbed the steps to our front door. "You don't have to integrate anymore."

"Well, praise the Lord," Grandma India said, her arms wide open to receive me. "You see, you made it." She squeezed me and kissed my cheek.

"Well, well, young lady, welcome to summer." Mother Lois handed me a large box that I rushed to open. "You're very special to have come through all this. I thought you deserved a special summer outfit."

Early on Wednesday morning, I built a fire in the metal trash barrel in the backyard, fueled by my school papers. Grandma had said it would **be healing** to write and destroy all the names of people I disliked at Central High: teachers, students, anyone who I thought had wronged me. It was against the law to burn anything at that time of the year, but she said a ceremony was important in order to **have the official opportunity to give that year to God**. Grandma India stood silent by my side as I fed the flame and spoke their names and forgave them.

....

punctuated interrupted

be healing make me feel better

have the official opportunity to give that year to God let go of what happened by praying to God

After a long moment she walked over to water her flowerbed. The four o'clocks were blooming purple and red. We stood together for what must have been half an hour, with only the sound of the crackling fire and the garden hose. Finally she said, "Later, you'll be grateful for the courage it built inside you and for the blessing it will bring."

Grateful, I thought. Never. How could I be grateful for being at Central High? But I knew she was always right. Still I wondered just how long I would have to wait for that feeling of gratitude to come to me.

Even though I had made it through the school year, Ernie still had to survive one final brave act—graduation. I counted on being with him, on applauding for him from our isolated though well-guarded section of the audience.

"None of you will be allowed to attend either **the graduation commencement or the baccalaureate service**," Mother Lois announced over dinner. "The authorities believe it would not only risk your lives, but also make it more difficult for them to protect Ernie and his family should they have to do so. They've also forbidden any nonwhite reporters or photographers to attend."

"But, Mom!"

"But nothing. This is no time to satisfy a **whim and unravel** everything you've accomplished. There'll be **enough of a circus**, what with the soldiers, FBI, city police, and who knows all."

....

the graduation commencement or the baccalaureate service of the graduation ceremonies

whim and unravel selfish desire and undo

enough of a circus a huge crowd

"The paper says every policeman not on vacation will be on duty from six o'clock on," Grandma said. "They wouldn't go to all that trouble and expense unless they expected something to happen."

"Besides," Mother Lois continued, "their best efforts should be directed to protecting Ernie."

She's right, I thought to myself. It was selfish of me to want to go, I suppose. But what I knew to be practical advice didn't lessen my disappointment at not being able to watch Ernie march triumphantly to the stage to receive that diploma. That night I wrote in my diary:

> *Dear God,*
>   *Please walk with Ernie in the graduation line at Central. Let him be safe.*

Quigley Stadium was where the 101st troops set up their headquarters. It was there, on Tuesday evening, May 27, with 4,500 people looking on, that Ernie received his diploma. I **held my breath** as I listened to the radio broadcast news of the graduation ceremonies. At 8:48 P.M., Ernie became the first of our people to graduate from Central High School in all its forty-nine years. **Chills danced up my spine** as I sat in the big green living room chair with Mama and Grandma nearby. "It really happened," I whispered. "We made it."

The audience had been applauding those who previously marched, but when Ernie appeared they fell silent.

....

held my breath was both nervous and excited

Chills danced up my spine I was excited and felt the importance of the event

"**What the heck**," Mother Lois said. "Lots of people in the rest of the world are applauding for Ernie and for all of you who made it through this year."

Ernie was escorted from the stadium by police to a waiting taxi in which he, his family, and their guest departed. The newspapers said Ernie's diploma cost taxpayers half a million dollars. Of course, we knew it cost all of us much, much more than that. It cost us our innocence and a precious year of our teenage lives.

The next morning Link called, sounding as though he **would fall apart**. He was grieving because Mrs. Healey had died on the day of his graduation. He insisted I come to meet him. When I said I couldn't get away, he called me a thousand times that day insisting he had to see me or something awful would happen.

Late that afternoon I had no choice but to meet him. He threatened to come right over to my house if I didn't agree. I figured I had to quiet him down or he would **explode**. He seemed inconsolable and really crazy. So I said we could walk around the block near the Baptist college. It was a safe place for me in my own neighborhood. Besides, when I asked Mother if I could go to the Baptist college library with a friend, I wouldn't be telling a lie—at least, not altogether.

When I arrived, he was red-faced and teary-eyed, insisting that I go with him to the Northern town near Harvard University where he would attend college.

....

What the heck It does not matter
would fall apart was very upset
explode do something crazy

"I've thought about this a lot. I'm tired of worrying about you. What will you do when I'm gone?"

"I can't leave. I have to stay here and go back to Central," I argued. "Everything depends on it."

"You keep acting this way, girl, you are gonna get yourself killed. I told you, there's **a price on your head**. They have posters all over offering that money. They'll never let you come back next year."

On and on he went, talking loud and frightening me. To calm him down, I told him I'd think about running away to the North. But when I waved goodbye to him, I knew I would never, ever see him again, although I would remember him forever.

By May 29 the eight of us had flown off to Chicago to receive the Robert S. Abbot Award **conferred** by the Chicago *Defender* newspaper. I was so excited because Minnijean joined us there. It was the beginning of a **whirlwind tour** and another in the series of awards we received for "bravery and significant contributions to democracy."

In Little Rock we had been "niggers," but up North we were heroes and heroines. We were paraded across stages before adoring audiences, chauffeured about in limousines, and treated like royalty at luxurious hotels.

In New York we had suites at the Statler Hilton, took limos to Sardi's, and lunched with United Nations Secretary General Dag Hammarskjöld. We **hobnobbed** backstage with Lena Horne and Ricardo Montalban at their Broadway play, *Jamaica*.

....

a price on your head money offered for your death
conferred given
whirlwind tour quick tour of many cities
hobnobbed visited

In Washington, we had a private tour of the White House and posed on the steps of the Supreme Court with Mr. Thurgood Marshall.

In Cleveland we received the NAACP's highest honor, the Spingarn Medal. We received so many other awards in so many cities that I lost count after a while. The first time I was asked for my autograph, I was astonished; afterward I went to my room to practice a special signature.

But by late June, even as Minnijean and I were **whirling about** our hotel room, dressing to see Johnny Mathis, a man we thought of as a deity, Little Rock school integration was **unraveling**. On June 22, Federal Judge Lemley granted the school board's request for a stay in the integration order for Central High School, delaying it for three and a half years. The NAACP began a round of appeals up through the courts, trying to get us seven students back into Central High.

By September 1958 we had won our court battle. Armed with judgments in our favor, we prepared to reenter Central High. But Governor Faubus had the last word. He closed all of Little Rock's high schools. So we began the school year waiting for the law of the land to blast Mr. Faubus out of his stubborn trench.

I couldn't know then that I would spend the entire school year of 1958–59 in lonely isolation and despair—waiting **in vain**. We had come back home, to Little Rock, back to being called "niggers" by the segregationists and those "meddling children" by our own people. Our friends and neighbors resented not only

....

whirling about busy in
unraveling falling apart
in vain with little hope

the school closure but most especially the **negative economic impact our presence in that school had on our community**.

By that time, segregationists were squeezing the life out of the NAACP and the Bateses' newspaper, the *State Press*. Our people continued to lose their jobs, their businesses, and their homes as pressure was exerted to convince them to talk us into voluntarily withdrawing from Central High.

During those lonely days of what would have been my senior year, I waited for legislators and Faubus and the NAACP to resolve the entanglement that surrounded Central High's integration. As September days turned to late autumn, my world fell apart with the onset of Grandmother India's leukemia and her death on October 24. Ultimately, I was alone, at home, waiting to restart my life—waiting to live my teenage years.

By September 1959 we had waited as long as we could for Faubus to open the schools. The unrest in Little Rock and the **bounty on our heads** had by that time forced two of our seven families to move their homes away from that city forever. NAACP officials sent an announcement to chapters across the country, asking for families that would volunteer to give us **safe harbor** and support us in finishing our education.

I was fortunate enough to go to the Santa Rosa, California, home of Dr. George McCabe, a San Francisco State University professor, and his wife, Carol, and their four children. They were a family of politically conscious Quakers committed to racial equality. When I arrived I was frightened to see that they were white. But they became the loving, nurturing bridge over

....

negative economic impact our presence in that school had on our community money our community lost because of it

bounty on our heads reward for our deaths

safe harbor protection, shelter

which I walked to adulthood.

More than their guidance, it was their unconditional love that taught me the true meaning of equality. To this day I call them Mom and Pop and visit to bask in their love and enjoy the privilege of being treated as though I am their daughter.

The love of George and Carol McCabe helped to heal my wounds and inspired me to launch a new life for myself. It was also their voices echoing the same words of my mother that made me enter and complete college. In fact, George took me to college in January, 1960, to register for my first classes.

Not until September, 1960, did the NAACP, with its **tenacious** legal work, force Central High to open to integration once more—but only two black students were permitted entry. Carlotta Walls and Jefferson Thomas ultimately became graduates of Central along with Ernest Green.

It would take years of **sorting out** my Central High experience before the pieces of my life puzzle would come together and I could make sense of what happened to me.

In 1962, when I had attended the mostly white San Francisco State University for two years, I found myself living among an enclave of students where I was the only person of color. I was doing it again, integrating a previously all-white residence house, even though I had other options. I had been taken there as a guest, and someone said the only blacks allowed there were the cooks. So, of course, I made application and **donned my warrior garb** because it reminded me of the **forbidden fences** of segregation in Little Rock.

....

tenacious persistent, continuous
sorting out thinking about; reflecting on
donned my warrior garb decided to fight once again
forbidden fences challenges

One night a brown-haired soldier wearing olive-drab fatigues stepped across the threshold of my suite. His name was John, and he was a blind date for Mary, my roommate. Of course, for just an instant, he reminded me of my 101st guard—same stature, same uniform. When he tried to talk to me that evening, I ignored him. But the next morning, Saturday, he rang our doorbell. When I told him that Mary had already left, John said **never mind**, he'd really come back to see me.

He brought me strawberries in dead of winter and flowers every weekend. Six months later I had married this bright, kind, green-eyed martial arts expert, who said he would protect me forever. Later I would come to understand that he represented Danny, my 101st guard; Link, my protector; the power of those who **held sway over** me at Central High; and the safety that my black uncles and father could not provide in the South.

"If you can't beat them, you're going to join them," my mother said when I nervously announced my wedding from a phone booth in Reno. "I hope you've thought this over, young lady. It's not the racial difference, it's the **philosophical difference** that is most important."

Seven years later John and I split up because he had been a farm boy who wanted a wife to **putter about** the house and have babies. I wanted to be a news reporter. But he had by then shared with me the most wonderful event in my life, the birth of our daughter, Kellie. As I held the cinnamon-colored bundle with auburn hair and doelike eyes in my arms, I swore she

....

never mind it did not matter

held sway over controlled

philosophical difference different beliefs you have

putter about take care of

would never have to endure the racial prejudices I endured. I was wrong. But then that's a story for another book.

Until my marriage I had been hearing from my old friend Link, living in faraway places as he piled up awards and degrees from this country's most prestigious educational institutions. He was livid about my marriage, saying I'd all along told him we couldn't date because he was white, and now look what I'd gone and done. I never heard from him again. Still, I think of him as a hero, yet another one of those special gifts from God sent to **ferry me over** a rough spot in my life's path.

Indeed, I followed my dream, inspired by those journalists I met during the integration. I attended Columbia University's School of Journalism and became a news reporter. I always remembered it was the truth told by those reporters who came to Little Rock that kept me alive. Later as an NBC television reporter covering stories of riot and protest, I would take special care to look into those **unexposed** corners where otherwise invisible people are forced to hide **as their truth is ignored**.

I look back on my Little Rock integration experience as ultimately a positive force that shaped the course of my life. As Grandma India promised, it taught me to have courage and patience.

My Central High School experience also taught me that we are not separate. The effort to separate ourselves whether by race, **creed**, color, religion, or status is as costly to the separator as to those who would be separated.

....

ferry me over help me through
unexposed hidden
as their truth is ignored because no one listens to them
creed beliefs

When the milk in Oregon is **tainted** by the radiation eruption of a Soviet nuclear reactor, we are forced to see **our interdependence**. When forgotten people feel compelled to riot in Los Angeles, we share their pain through our TV screens, and their **ravages impact** our emotional and economic health.

The task that remains is to cope with our interdependence —to see ourselves reflected in every other human being and to respect and honor our differences.

Namasté
(the God in me sees and honors the God in you)

---

tainted ruined
our interdependence how we are all connected
ravages impact pain and destruction affect

Epilogue:
Little Rock Warriors
Thirty Years Later

THE LITTLE ROCK NINE COME TOGETHER
FOR THE FIRST TIME SINCE '57
—*Arkansas Gazette*, Friday, October 23, 1987

The stone steps are slippery with morning **drizzle** as we begin
the **tedious** climb up to the front door of Central High School.
It is the first time in thirty years that we nine black **alumni**
have entered this school together.

On this day Arkansas Governor Billy Clinton, who in less
than six years will be President of the United States, greets us
warmly with a welcoming smile as he extends his hand. We
are honored guests, celebrating both our reunion and thirty
years of progress in Little Rock's race relations. Cameras flash,
reporters shout questions, **dignitaries** lavish enthusiastic praise

....

drizzle rain
tedious long
alumni former students
dignitaries important people

257

on us, and fans ask for our autographs.

And yet all this **pomp and circumstance** and the presence of my eight colleagues does not numb the pain I feel at entering Central High School, a building I remember only as a hellish torture chamber. I pause to look up at this massive school—two blocks square and seven stories high, a place that was meant to nourish us and prepare us for adulthood. But because we dared to challenge the Southern tradition of segregation, this school became, instead, a **furnace that consumed our youth and forged us into reluctant warriors**.

On this occasion, we nine ascend the stairs amid a group of reporters and dignitaries gathered here for the National Association for the Advancement of Colored People convention.

"How does it feel to be in Little Rock again?" a reporter shouts.

"Weird," I reply.

We nine have come from our homes around the world. Gloria, a magazine publisher, is a citizen of the Netherlands. Minnijean, a Canadian citizen, is a writer and raises her six children on a farm. Shearson Lehman Hutton V.P. Ernie comes from New York; Thelma has come from her Illinois teaching duties; and Dr. Terry Roberts comes from his UCLA professor's post. Carlotta is a Denver realtor, and Jeff is a Defense Department accountant from California. Only Elizabeth stayed on in Little Rock, where she is a social worker. It is **significant** that almost all of us chose not to remain in Little Rock but sought lives elsewhere.

....

pomp and circumstance honoring of us, ceremony

furnace that consumed our youth and forged us into reluctant warriors place that took our innocence and made us fighters

significant important

All of us bring children—some are adults now like my daughter, Kellie. Others are toddlers, or the same age as we were when we attended Central.

Our relationships with one another and the joy of our **camaraderie** have not changed. For me our reunion has been a rediscovery of a part of myself that was lost—a part that I longed to **be in touch with**. I have missed these eight people who **by virtue of fate's hand** are most dear to me. Since our arrival in Little Rock, we have laughed and cried together and talked nonstop. We have both relished and dreaded this moment when we would again walk up these stairs.

Today, if I let the memories flood in and listen closely, on these same stone steps I can hear the click-clack of leather boots—boots worn by soldiers of the 101st Airborne, dispatched to escort us past the raging mob. I hear the raspy voices of their leaders commanding, "Forward march," as we first walked through these front doors on September 25, 1957.

"What was it like to attend Central?" asks one reporter.

"I got up every morning, polished my saddle shoes, and went off to war," I reply. "It was like being a soldier on a battlefield."

"It was a teenager's worst nightmare," someone else shouts. "What's worse than to be rejected by all your classmates and teachers."

"How does the city look to you now?"

I answer the question to myself. Very different from when I lived here. Today I could not find my way around its newly built freeways, its thriving **industrial complexes**, its racially mixed,

....

camaraderie friendship and loyalty
be in touch with remember
by virtue of fate's hand by chance; by God's choice
industrial complexes businesses and factories

upscale **suburban sprawl**. It is a town that now boasts a black woman mayor. My brother, Conrad, is the first and only black captain of the Arkansas State Troopers—the same troopers that held me at bay as a teenager when I tried to enter Central.

We reach the crest of the first bank of stairs, turn right at the landing, and begin mounting the next set of steps when we hear more shouting from the reporters: "Stop. Look this way, please. Can you wave?"

Where is Governor Faubus, I wonder. Where is the man who dispatched armed soldiers to keep nine children out of school, who bet his life and his career that he could halt integration?

"Faubus is quoted on the news wires today saying if he had it to do over again, he'd do the same thing. What do you think about that?" a reporter asks.

"If we had it to do again, we'd do the same," Terry **quips**.

"Why isn't Faubus here?" someone asks.

"Because he wasn't invited," a reporter replies. "At least that's what he says. He retired to some small town in Arkansas."

All at once, I realize the questions have suddenly stopped. I am surrounded by an anxious silence—like the hush of an audience **as the curtain is about to rise**. The main entrance of the school is now clearly in sight. I feel a familiar **twinge**; a cold fist clamps about my stomach and twists it into a wrenching knot, and just at that instant, it is October of 1957, and I am a helpless, frightened fifteen-year-old, terrified of what awaits me behind those doors. What will they do to me

....

suburban sprawl neighborhoods

quips says

as the curtain is about to rise before a play begins

twinge feeling, emotion

today? Will I make it to my homeroom? Who will be the first to slap me, to kick me in the shin, or call me nigger?

Suddenly one of the huge front doors swings open. A black teenager **impeccably** dressed in morning coat and bow tie emerges. He is slight, perhaps five feet six inches tall, with closely cropped hair, wearing wire-rimmed spectacles. He bows slightly as we approach.

"Good morning. I am Derrick Noble, president of the student **body**. Welcome to Central High School."

---

impeccably neatly
body government

BEFORE YOU MOVE ON...

1. **Sequence** Reread pages 252–253. Little Rock closed all of the high schools. What happened to Melba next?

2. **Generalization** Reread pages 257–261. Why are stories like Melba's important?